THE SWEDISH PROPHET

Swedenborg Studies No. 20

T0350744

THE SWEDISH PROPHET

*Reflections on the Visionary Philosophy
of Emanuel Swedenborg*

José Antonio Antón-Pacheco

Translated by Steven Skattebo

Swedenborg Foundation Press
West Chester, Pennsylvania

Swedenborg Studies is a scholarly series published by the Swedenborg Foundation. The primary purpose of the series is to make materials available for understanding the life and thought of Emanuel Swedenborg (1688–1772) and the impact his thought has had on others. The Foundation undertakes to publish original studies, English translations of such studies, and primary sources that are otherwise difficult to access.
Proposals should be sent to: Editor, Swedenborg Foundation, 320 North Church Street, West Chester, PA 19380.

Library of Congress Cataloging-in-Publication Data
Antón Pacheco, José Antonio.
[Profeta del norte. English]
The Swedish prophet : reflections on the visionary philosophy of Emanuel Swedenborg / José Antonio Antón Pacheco ; translated by Steven Skattebo.
p. cm. — (Swedenborg studies)
Includes bibliographical references (p.   ) and index.
ISBN 978-0-87785-342-8 (alk. paper)
1. Swedenborg, Emanuel, 1688-1772. 2. Philosophy. 3. Philosophical theology. I. Title.
B4468.S84A65 2012
289'.4092—dc23
2011047713

Edited by Morgan Beard
Design and typesetting by Karen Connor

Printed in the United States of America

Swedenborg Foundation Press
320 North Church Street
West Chester, PA 19380
www.swedenborg.com

*Since the publication of the first version of this book in 1991,
I have received important assistance on this topic from
Karl-Erik Sjödén, Lars Bergquist, Christen Blom-Dahl, and
Leonard Fox, to whom I give my thanks.*

But my deepest gratitude is for Maribel.

CONTENTS

PREFACE

It is difficult to do justice to the complex and enthralling human and intellectual figure of Emanuel Swedenborg within the narrow limits of a prologue. Nevertheless, a preview of this Swedish visionary's work becomes necessary, given that it is little or poorly known among us. This is not to say that our treatment here will remediate these deficiencies. We simply want to contribute some information that will help us to better understand the man called the Prophet of the North. We will avoid Swedenborg's biographical details, which, though they are important, at times superimpose themselves anecdotally over his actual work.

The figure of Swedenborg presents us with a paradigm of a certain philosophical and theological attitude. Indeed, a phenomenological analysis of Swedenborg's work would show how a variety of philosophical, theological, and mythical themes are expressed in an exemplary manner, themes that are consistent within a certain line of thought. This line of thought is at the same time easy and difficult to define. Easy, because its characteristics stand out so much at first sight that immediately we discern them and we define them in relation to other currents. Difficult, because its internal complexity makes its analysis—historical as well as phenomenological—fairly arduous. We are simply saying that we refer to currents that fall within areas such as mysticism or spiritual hermeneutics. As will be shown, these designations are rather problematic in themselves and they will need clarification, requiring us to enter into Swedenborg's thought. We will see the constants that are revealed in the history of this type of thought, and we will show how these constants are found one way or another in Swedenborg (naturally, without detriment to the originality of our author). We affirm that the Scandinavian thinker is a paradigm of a certain philosophy of religion, because in him we find a great deal from the same philosophical/religious categories mentioned above.

Accordingly, Swedenborg will serve as a reference point to begin a study of religious philosophy and comparative spiritual hermeneutics, fields where, we reiterate, Swedenborg is a privileged paradigm. And together with all these elements mentioned, one must keep in mind Swedenborg's formative components: his illustrious training as a scientist and his Christian reformative thrust. All these factors have to be considered if we want a true idea of Swedenborg's thought.

We are proposing a continuity and a harmonization among the spiritual currents that have appeared in the history of religious consciousness. But such continuity and harmonization are not necessarily due to genetics or historical succession; first one must view them as an emergence of common archetypes and symbols together with common perceptions and experiences. This will be our line of study in this examination of Swedenborg's works: we will analyze some categories that appear in religious and exegetical philosophies and we will compare them with those of Swedenborg.

One methodological issue is essential from the beginning: we will approach Swedenborg according to the standards of a type of thought that frequently utilizes mythical vehicles of expression. Therefore, Swedenborg will have to be treated with the same methodological criteria that are applied to other systems with mythical traits. Otherwise, the result will be the usual misunderstanding of Swedenborg. This means it will be necessary to demythologize the Scandinavian visionary, which does not imply a demystification or the reductionism of a rationalist "criticism"; it means, rather, the translation of mythic forms to the more comprehensive schema provided by the phenomenology of religion and by a comparative analysis of the diverse modalities of religious consciousness. The lack of sensibility regarding Swedenborg to which we alluded before has been caused precisely by a lack of perspective when analyzing his work. If we keep in mind that we need to place Swedenborg's vision alongside visions that are, for example, prophetic, apocalyptic, and gnostic, we therefore need to employ the same method of investigation toward him as toward those visions. Only if we add to these factors those equally important factors of scientific training and the critical impulse of a Christian reformer can we penetrate into Swedenborg's spiritual world.

All in all, it is a matter of translating a form of speech that has its own internal dynamic to another language—ours—so that the experiences expressed can be transmitted and understood by us. It is about interpreting, about phenomenalizing Swedenborg's ontological horizon into our own ontological horizon. We need to apply to Swedenborg the same hermeneutics we apply to the phenomena that show a spiritual affinity with our author. The description of such spiritual events and the comparative analysis of its elements—elements that are experiences of the soul—give us guidelines as to which hermeneutics we need to follow in order to interpret Swedenborg, while they simultaneously indicate the place of the Swedish thinker among similar spiritual currents.

Swedenborg was an author living between the seventeenth and eighteenth centuries, but the type of experience that he relates to us in his books, the symbolism described in his visions, the theosophical base that underlies his literary output, present us with a morphology so similar to that of all the great visionary texts and theosophical experiences—whatever be their time and place—that they lead us to affirm the validity of Swedenborg's inner life under the universal models of many great mystics and theosophists. The philosophy of religion revealed in Swedenborg's thought occupies a space that contains motifs of the Enochian cycle and of Neoplatonic metaphysics, Dante and Ibn 'Arabi, Sohravardi and the Zohar. All these are inextricably united with the other dominant factors in the wise Swede's system: the scientific element and the element of Christian reformation, which lend an existential tenor to the whole system, as we will see later. Therefore, the crucial components in this line of religious and existential philosophy, its constant archetypes, will also be the crucial components of Swedenborg's work, and the hermeneutical approach must be similar for all of them.

Accordingly, could we affirm that Swedenborg states in a more or less mythic manner what Hamann, for example, states in a theological manner with respect to spiritual hermeneutics, or Philo of Alexandria affirms in a philosophical manner with respect to the idea of Logos, or Unamuno maintains about the existential character of the human being? There is something to this. In fact, our interpretation of the wise Swede points to it: we aim to make clear that the themes he deals with are the same ones that others have dealt with in either a similar or a different parlance. However, it is also necessary to keep in mind two things: firstly, we should not exaggerate the mythical components in Swedenborg's work; in fact, there are far fewer mythemes than is usually thought, and many of the ideas can only be explained from the scientific, Enlightenment-based parameters in which Swedenborg is grounded. Secondly, we need to recognize that language and content are united, such that the utilization of a certain way of speaking conditions the content expressed. By this we mean to say that an experiential specificity exists in Swedenborg, one based on the meaning that he communicates to us and on the expressive channel that leads to such a meaning. One cannot abandon the mythic component of Swedenborg without undermining the fundamental core of his thought (and neither can one abandon any of the other components). All these motifs lend Swedenborg's work its seal of irreducible and integral experience; and the mythic form is part of that same spiritual experience. A demythologizing of Swedenborg surely provides us with some clarity about his ideas, but also it is certain that the demythologizing takes away much of the vital and individual richness of Swedenborg's thought. In this respect, our proposition is the same as that of Karl Kerényi and his lucid words about the Greek people: "[The Hellene] reflects a world that he contemplates with eyes wide open and full of spirit—or he projects his open eye and his spirit over the world. Call it what you will! The role of our science is not to keep on tearing apart the unity that has been dissolved for a long time, but rather to comprehend it."[1] Indeed, this is the aim of all hermeneutics, and this is the aim that we propose in our study of Swedenborg: preserve the unity that he assumes and bring its presence into our own sphere, and make his language speak through and by means of our own language. We accept the limitations that such a method implies, but we certainly do not forsake the search for a spiritual phenomenon in all its integrity.

Finally, we want to express that this present study aims to be not just a monograph about the Nordic philosopher, but also an exposition of our own thought, a thought that is clearly marked by Swedenborg's footprint. Therefore, one should not look for a purely and simply intellectual intention, but above all a more profound, more vital, more inclusive motivation. In the end, we must always have Swedenborg's vision as a support and guiding principle, since ultimately our aim is to show that Swedenborg's entire monumental work is the result of a deep spiritual experience.

THE SWEDISH PROPHET

INTRODUCTION

The scarce and distorted information about the life of Emanuel Swedenborg makes it necessary to include some brief biographical and bibliographical notes, which will clear the way toward the comprehension of the Prophet of the North. Emanuel Swedenborg, son of renowned bishop and theologian Jesper Svedberg, was born in Stockholm in 1688 and died in London in 1772. He studied humanities at the University of Uppsala, where he presented the thesis *Lucio Annaei Senecae et Pubio Syri Mimi, forsam et aliorum Selectiae Sententiae (Selected Sentences from L. Annaeus Seneca and Publius [Publilius] Syrus the Mime).* We have an example of his humanistic vocation in the Latin poems he wrote (Swedenborg wrote almost all of his immense body of work in Latin): *Ludus Heliconius (Heliconian Pastimes), Festivus Applausus (Joyous Accolades),* and *Camena Borea (Northern Muse).* But very soon Swedenborg began to take an interest in science. In this respect and to keep abreast of the scientific knowledge of his era, Swedenborg embarked on a series of trips to England, France, Holland, and Germany. On those trips he studied Newton and Malebranche, and personally met the astronomers Flamsteed, Halley, Philippe de la Hire, and other eminent scientists of the period. In Swedenborg's scientific training one must keep in mind the influence of the wise Erik Benzelius, his brother-in-law; that of Linnaeus, his uncle; and that of the inventor Christophen Polhem, with whom Swedenborg collaborated. Swedenborg promoted Polhem's inventions through *Daedalus Hyperboreus* (1716–18), a magazine financed by Swedenborg himself.

Swedenborg's interest in science extended to practically all the spheres of knowledge of his age: astronomy, geology, mineralogy, anatomy, engineering (he was employed at the royal Board of Mines). His scientific work is enormous. Between 1716 and 1745 he published, among other texts: *Principia Rerum Naturalium* (*Basic Principles of Nature,* also translated *Philosophical and Mineralogical Works;* three volumes, Dresden and Leipzig, 1734), *Prodromus Philosophiae Ratiocinantis de Infinito, et Causa Finali Creationis* (*The Infinite and Final Cause of Creation;* Dresden, 1734), *Oeconomia Regni Animalis* (*Economy of the Animal Kingdom,* also translated *Dynamics of the Soul's Domain;* two volumes, Amsterdam, 1740–41), and *Regnum Animale* (*The Animal Kingdom,* also translated *The Soul's Domain;* three volumes, The Hague, 1744–45). Swedenborg's scientific thought belonged in principle to the mechanistic Cartesian school, but from 1730 on Swedenborg's thinking began to evolve as he questioned that mechanistic view, concerned with the relationship between soul and body and with the possible connection between nature and spiritual principles. This scientific issue progressively led him to an interest in theology and psychology, concluding with a religious crisis in 1741. We want to highlight the evolutionary character of Swedenborg's spiritual transformation, because it demonstrates that this transformation was not due to any instantaneous, rare, or strange phenomenon. There is not a first Swedenborg who is scientific and a second one who is a visionary—in fact, he publishes a scientific work after his decisive inner experience of 1743–44— but rather the progressive maturation of a growing philosophical/ religious uneasiness. Between 1743 and 1744 the crisis that started years earlier is consummated, and the existential experience that had been germinating in Swedenborg reaches its peak: we have a chronicle of this situation in his dream diary (see chapter 6). Soon afterward, our author dedicates himself completely to his theological work, as immense as his body of scientific writings: *De Cultu et Amore Dei* (*Worship and Love of God;* London, 1745), where he already clearly shows his attraction to biblical exegesis; *Arcana Coelestia* (*Secrets of Heaven;* eight volumes, London, 1749–56), a principal work from which he took sections and published them as separate volumes; *De Coelo et Ejus Mirabilibus, et de Inferno* (*On Heaven and Its Wonders, and Hell,* more commonly known as *Heaven and Hell;* London, 1758), *Sapientia Angelica de Divino Amore et de Divina Sapientia* (*Angelic Wisdom about Divine Love and Divine Wisdom,* more commonly known as *Divine Love and Wisdom;* Amsterdam, 1763). We end our summary, so as not to make an excessive catalog of his works, with the important *Vera Christiana Religio* (*True Christianity;* Amsterdam, 1771), the last book published by Swedenborg during his life and an excellent and straightforward compendium of his theological doctrine.

We will not yet begin a concrete analysis of Swedenborg's works, nor of any of their contents; we will expand on those topics, at least in part, later in this book. At this point we will examine only the influence of Swedenborg on Romanticism, on literary symbolism, and on a great many authors.[1] In our times the most faithful interpreters have been Ernst Benz and above all Henry Corbin, who has provided us a truer picture of Swedenborg by applying phenomenology and comparative hermeneutics to his works. With respect to the common misconceptions that circulate about Swedenborg, we can state the following: he never founded an actual church (the constitution of the New Church was a task of his disciples); he never had any relations with esoteric fraternities such as the Illuminati of Avignon that guided Antoine-Joseph Pernety (the first translator of Swedenborg into French); he never belonged to any Masonic lodge, the so-called Swedenborgian Rite being completely alien to him. In short, he was never in contact with the occultist groups that were common in his era.[2] On the contrary: he explicitly criticized the belief in miracles and all types of divination. His interest rested on going back to an inner religiosity that for him, as for so many radical reformers, was found in a return to pre-Nicene Christianity.[3]

1

UNITY AND DETERMINATION
IN SWEDENBORG

The poles around which this study revolves are unity and determination. Unity, because this is the constant that moves all of Swedenborg's thought and vital experience. Determination, because despite appearances this search for unity is not resolved in an abstract and absolute unitarianism, but rather is particularized and concretized in the multiple and varied richness of reality. In short, for Swedenborg, "being is one, but it is stated in many forms." Being is determination; but it is lived religiously—we could even say mystically, existentially.

The basis of Swedenborg's system is the verification of unity as a condition that makes all of reality possible. But this metaphysical requirement does not derive from a conceptual or purely intellectual analysis; the ontological unity of reality is above all Swedenborg's inner experience. That is, the necessity to postulate unity as a fundamental category stems from an effort to overcome Cartesian dualism. That reasoning produced a world of dualities, as much on the intellectual and scientific planes as in the plane of the most vivid inner world. The result was a divided consciousness that saw a split reality: science/religion, soul/body, God/world, reason/faith, and so on. All of Swedenborg's philosophy, science, and technology is directed against this dual, schism-filled vision; and he endeavors, furthermore, to establish ontological connection and unity in a world that he experienced as painfully divided. Here we have the true motivation behind Swedenborg's work and his hermeneutical key: the overcoming of Cartesian dualism and the postulation of unity as fundamental sustenance of and bond between all the levels of existence. As noted earlier, the holistic category is not predicated simply to resolve questions of a philosophical or scientific nature (which would be the case of the binomials body/soul and matter/spirit), but also to resolve problems that are more inner, more spiritual. These dualities affect not only the mind that scientifically scrutinizes reality, but also, foremost, the consciousness, which is seen as tragically split. Here we find a great similarity between the existential assumptions of Swedenborg and Pascal. Pascal expressed a painful awareness of the opposition of contrary positions; in the Frenchman we find the need to discover a connection between those opposites, fundamentally in respect to the dualities that most vitally affect human beings, that is, the dualities that provoke the split of consciousness. Naturally, in Swedenborg the solution to this situation is different from Pascal's, but the existential approach allows us to position Swedenborg within the spiritual affiliation that includes Pascal himself, Kierkegaard, Unamuno, and Berdyaev.[1]

As stated earlier, in Swedenborg the overcoming of dualism and the postulation of unity take on two aspects: one that refers to dualities of a scientific type and one that refers to those of a religious or existential nature. Moreover, the same duality that shapes those two aspects also needs to be resolved under the category of unity, in this way obtaining a totalizing vision of reality. Such is the Swedenborgian project. And this project is carried to all spheres.

As a result, what Swedenborg seeks is the connection between the different ontological levels of reality. It is about establishing a unifying bridge between the intelligible and the perceptible and their different determinations. The division that first seems to Swedenborg more incisive is that of the body and soul, as this dichotomy has to account for the relationship between the corporeal and the spiritual and of their mutual influence, and this same dichotomy drastically separates the inner and outer worlds. In the theoretical and practical desire to reconcile these opposites we have to look at the correspondences that Swedenborg, in one phase of his thought, established between the spiritual worlds and the natural spheres. What Swedenborg wants to show is the ontological solidarity that exists between body and spirit, inner and outer worlds, humans and nature, and, if we extend this reasoning, between God and the world. Here, in our judgment, lies the philosophical and theological system of the wise Swede. It is a matter of overcoming the breach that all dualism introduces into reality, with the resulting metaphysical and epistemological difficulties that arise from it: How does the body influence and coordinate with the soul, being radically different substances? How does the intelligible inform and make contact with the perceptible? How does God rejoin the world if the ontological separation *(jorismós)* is bottomless? However, it is also a matter of reconciling the body with the soul, the human with the world, the world with God. All in all, it is about recognizing the diversified unity that is existence.

For Swedenborg there is no division or ontological breach in the stages of being, and to explain this he turns to the full range of concepts and figures that traditional thought has utilized to such effect: correspondences, representations, catoptrics, participation, reflection, and so on. The whole universe finds itself thus reunited and ontologically connected, and each of its parts are reflected in all parts, and all parts are reflected in each one, thus resulting in a metaphysical solidarity of all beings. The intelligible world itself, which in the religious language of Swedenborg is equivalent to the divine world and to God himself, has its correspondences in the perceptible world, bringing about the presence of the divine in the world, a presence that ultimately puts this metaphysical unity into effect in the perceptible world.[2] And the human being himself (as *omnia fabrica, mezorios,* or *adunatio*) becomes a mirror that captures the reflections of other spheres and itself reflects them; that is, the human being has his correspondences with the intelligible regions and the perceptible worlds. Hence the human being feels at one with the world, recognizes himself in external reality, and finds himself tied more intimately to all other beings. We have already stated that here lies one of the reasons that Romantics and symbolists have such a fascination with Swedenborg: the visionary Swede systematizes the universal symbolism through which the human being represents everything and is seen represented in everything. But it is not only the aesthetic component implied by this systematization of universal representations and correspondences that attracts Romantics, symbolists, and those spirits with refined religious sensibilities. It is above all the role that the human being acquires as a supportive element to the rest of the universe and to God that attracted so many personalities, especially in an era in which humans were breaking ties with Divinity and with the cosmos.

Following this line of thought, we can infer that for Swedenborg the human is a being from top to bottom, that is, a being that occupies—or can occupy—all the levels of reality, from the material to the intelligible or spiritual; and the human is also a being whose most radical possibility is precisely the power to open himself to all those levels, of being able to convert himself into them. The human is mediation and means of union of all these levels.[3]

However, the unity that, according to Swedenborg, shines in everything real as a condition of its very possibility does not belong only to the ontological sphere. In the human being there are other instantiations overseen by the category of unity. We refer now to the science/faith dichotomy. Just as ontological and epistemological dichotomies impeded a homogenous vision of the human being and the world, provoking, on the contrary, irreducible divisions, so now the duality of science and faith raises issues in the field of religious belief. We need to look at the closeness and dependency of these two spheres (the ontological-epistemological and that of religious belief), since the Cartesian dualism that led to mechanism involved a rethinking, if not a nullification, of the spiritual and religious initiatives of the human being. The resolution of the dichotomy that split reality was to place God as a *tertium comparationis* (the third part of the comparison) between the body and the soul and between humans and the cosmos, that is, as a connecting link between the material and the intelligible, and as a universal bond between everything created. It is logical, then, that there is a strong, underlying, existential purpose in the problems that originate in the science/faith relationship. In his treatment of this matter Swedenborg shows that he is a man of the Enlightenment: he wants to enlighten minds and hearts to make them see the truth of Christian doctrine.[4] But the means of resolving the dichotomy do not lie in a rationalistic reduction of faith. What is of fundamental interest for us now is to consider the following: First, here as in other fields, Swedenborg seeks unity in the face of a duality that to him appears artificial. Second, his interest is apologetic, wanting to show how it is possible that there is no contradiction between science and faith. Third, this attitude owes much to the wise Swede's grounding in the Enlightenment. What Swedenborg does is extrapolate his scientific vision to his theological vision, dissolving the breach between them. Emerson saw this in his essay on Swedenborg in *Representative Men*. There is not any split at all between the scientific Swedenborg and the theological Swedenborg. In fact, what the Scandinavian does is transfer the structures of the natural to the structures of the spiritual. He does this not by virtue of a disguised materialism, but rather because of an impulse that leads him to find a spiritual footprint or presence in all of reality. In Swedenborg there are always underlying motifs of Enlightenment thought and innermost Christian experience.[5]

We must reiterate that we are not dealing with a rationalistic reduction of faith to science; rather, what is happening is that Swedenborg does not conceive of any part, element, or sphere of reality in an isolated or independent manner. Instead, for Swedenborg all entities find themselves in mutual correspondence, and each sphere or realm has its correspondence in the different states or realms of being. The same thing happens with religious belief: the contents of this sphere are clarified by the epistemological and rational parameters used by Swedenborg. Here the biblical hermeneutics utilized by the Swedish thinker are very important. All of Swedenborg's ontological examples have a connection with biblical hermeneutics and are applicable to them. Thus a relationship is established between ontology, anthropology, and hermeneutics, which is typical of this type of thought, but Swedenborg adds the term natural science to this confirmed relationship. The issue of spiritual exegesis of the revealed Book overlaps with the similarities between macrocosm and microcosm (see *Divine Love and Wisdom* §206). In short, what Swedenborg always seeks in his investigations is the link that reunites and binds together all the spheres of reality, thus avoiding the metaphysical dispersion, disunity, and isolation of these spheres.

But the unitary and totalizing conception of being and of entities does not lead Swedenborg to see the world as an abstract unity in which the contrasts and the diversity of pluralities dissolve and disappear; far from it. In Swedenborg unity does not annul the qualitative richness of plurality, but rather the contrary, since there is no substantive reduction of ontological plurality to the supreme category of unity; thus there is in Swedenborg neither acosmism (a denial of the existence of the universe) nor pantheism. In effect, if unity is one of the fundamental poles of Swedenborg's worldview, the other pole is the category of determination, or, stated in Swedenborg's words: everything is "distinguishably one."[6] The ontological unity that causes everything to acquire its being and meaning, that makes everything stay connected and correlated—that unity is established in every representation and correspondence, and because they are established in unity, they receive being, meaning, and identity. Swedenborg thus gathers the two fundamental principles of philosophy: being is unity, being is determination.[7]

For Swedenborg determination is like a corollary of unity, and the same motives (philosophical, scientific, religious) that drive him to the postulation of unity likewise drive him to the position of determination. We have spoken of a mysticism of determination as an essential characteristic of Swedenborg's thought. Regarding this, we would like to mention the religious and ontological impulse through which all of reality advances in order to be determined—that is, to be itself, to acquire its being—and inasmuch as determination occurred, more being resulted. We can, then, speak of mysticism, since the process of determination of reality takes place thanks to a spiritual attempt *(conatus)*, effort *(nisum)*, and force *(vis)*. The determination itself is spirituality, the tendency toward spirituality. However, it must be understood that by the term mysticism we mean nothing similar to a bewildering confusion of the concrete in the Absolute, to a dissolving of plurality in abstractness, to a loss of ontological delimitation. Quite the reverse happens for Swedenborg: determination is to be this and this and this; it is pluralistic richness, metaphysical variety, the seminal capacity of being and fruitfulness. The same sense of determinism goes against any tendency or proclivity toward "a night when all cats are gray," that is, toward an informal and abstract unity that does not respect concrete plurality. For Swedenborg, being is being something; being is to be determined as this or that. There is no dispersion of the plurality of concrete determinations, because, as has already been stated, the unity of being keeps all the orders of reality bound and connected, and establishes an ontological continuity among all those levels so that they mutually correlate and reflect each other. For this reason, representation and correspondence are the two fundamental forms of determination. Therefore, from the point of view of unity, there is the possibility of solidarity and adaptation among all the spheres of nature, and among them, humans and God. From the perspective of determination, the abstract and impoverishing formalism to which all monism or totalitarian ontologism leads is avoided. Thus, we now proceed to clarify and specify the movement and development of the determinations. Above all, we state that the category of determination explains the development of Swedenborg's complex system, in which each thing (more precisely, each determination) acquires its meaning and its function in relation to the whole. At the same time it makes possible the dominant role that the sciences play in the balance of his thought, although naturally we must also consider that his scientific training significantly influenced his metaphysical considerations regarding the category of determination.

Once again, then, we draw attention to the two principal characteristics of Swedenborg's thought to which its internal structure refers. The category of unity is a consequence of harmonizing the totality of his scientific vision, his teleological system, and his religious-existential experience. The category of determination makes possible the epistemological pluralism and development of his scientific level, as well as the unfolding of the ontological individuality of all beings, and especially humans. But let us examine how determination is determined.

For Swedenborg, everything moves toward existence, toward manifesting itself, toward configuring itself, and ultimately, toward personifying itself; we believe this is the essential manner of determination in the Swedish thinker. Therefore, we can affirm that a thing has more existence the more determination it acquires, that is, the more it personalizes itself. If determination means that each thing is distinguishably one, what measures such distinction is personalization; effectively, the parameter of the person is what establishes a greater degree and a greater density of elements and individualizing and distinctive factors. A person is more differentiated than a rock, has more individual features, and therefore possesses more ontological density than a rock.

Thus, we see the important role of the human being for Swedenborg, and more specifically the angel, given that we can consider the figure of the angel to be simply the maximum statement of personalization, that is, of determination. An angel is the realization of the ontological and existential potential of the human being, its specific determination. The figure of the angel, then, represents the following: human beings experience a trend and tension toward their fullness; this trend has personalization as its goal, and that very fullness is personalization.

The category of determination is essentially articulated through two instantiations, which form something like the two pillars of Swedenborg's system: correspondence and representation. As stated earlier, because of these two terms reality is not an abstract unity, but rather an ordered and harmonious whole where all its elements configure and conform themselves, where lines of meaning are established that gather together the orders of ontological participation and similarity. This causes a universal catoptric in which the spheres of reality reflect through and because of the categories of correspondence and representation. The different ontological regions correspond in successive steps, and each region represents the previous region. In this fashion the whole of reality is determined, and this determination itself is the product of the whole of reality. Determination as correspondence and representation assumes a metaphysical factor that permits the participation and the imitation of all entities in supreme and transcendental moments, that is, in their archetypal models.[8] Thus we have a symbolic constellation where everything achieves its corresponding place in relation to the rest of reality, as is proper to traditional systems. In this sense, Swedenborg could be placed in the same line of thought that includes personalities such as Pseudo-Dionysius or John Scotus Eriugena, except that when Swedenborg constructs his system he utilizes the scientific knowledge of his era, which was, of course, authoritative.

This catoptric and symbolic vision in which unity and plurality are reconciled makes possible the presence of higher instantiations in the world below. In other words, determinations are themselves the very presence of the intelligible in reality. Thus, the dichotomies that for Swedenborg form a categorical and transcendental paradigm—Love/Wisdom, Good/Truth, Will/Understanding, Substance/Form, Being/Existing—are certainly the supreme determinations, since they are in

God himself. However, by virtue of the system of correspondences and representations they are present analogically in all phases of our reality. They are, in fact, what ontologically determines our reality. In this way, all areas of our reality represent, are, and contain love and wisdom, goodness and truth, etc. Therefore, the unity that was our world is articulated, distinguished, and determined by all the metaphysical categories that make unity distinguishably one; all is love and wisdom, in their respective spheres, and all participate in love and wisdom. That is to say, thanks to the participation of the higher determinations, the world connects with God and God makes himself present in the world. Each thing contains wholeness and wholeness is reflected in each thing; alternatively, the unity of all is the unity of each thing and the determinations of everything are the determinations of each thing. The conformity between the exterior and the interior, between the world and the soul, and between the material and the spiritual, then, is established by the order of determinations.

However, in Swedenborg there is a third essential determination that expresses two other characteristics that are fundamental to his thought. In effect, he adds a third instantiation to the Love/Wisdom binomial: Use. In a similar fashion, other fundamental dichotomies also have a third member: End/Cause/Effect, Affection/Thought/Action, Tendency/Force/Movement, and so on. All these third factors of the determinative relationship mean one thing: the ontological uniformity of Swedenborg. That is, all determinations strive toward realization; they all strive toward being and manifestation. Determinations derive their meaning from the effective embodiment that they carry out. It could be said that for Swedenborg, reality fulfills or reflects the Scholastic adage *operari sequitur esse* (action follows being). The ontological uniformity of Swedenborg causes all of reality to rest on a movement toward form, toward the full phenomenalization of all possibilities of being. Use, action, effect, and movement are all realizations of determinations, the fulfillment of the process that leads to the performance of its ontological role, which is to actualize the implicit or latent. This actualism is universal (as is everything in Swedenborg), since all the realms of the universe are an image of their Model, and if this is pure actuality, pure realization of being, in the same way each entity in particular and the world in its totality will also be seen as being driven toward their fulfillment. Therefore, the movement of reality as a whole and of each reality in particular is a movement toward the epiphany of being, toward being in action. It is a movement that carries with it the provision that nothing remains unformed, hidden, or latent, but rather that everything acquires form and configuration, that reality be revealed. And furthermore this unveiling occurs for Swedenborg on all levels of reality—as we have stated, what happens in a higher order happens also in all the other orders. In this way we understand the value of science for Swedenborg, inasmuch as science uncovers the mysteries of nature. There is also value in mystical biblical exegesis, inasmuch as biblical hermeneutics reveals the hidden meanings of the sacred text. The importance given to works is also understood (in the face of the Lutheran belief in salvation by faith alone), since works are what bring the powers and virtues of the human being into action.[9] Swedenborg is neither an obscurantist nor an occultist; for him being and reality are prone to manifestation in their most splendid complexity. Thus it is impossible to subsume Swedenborg in any movement of acosmist character, since for him the movement of being leads always to manifestation, realization, and determination, and his own works always deal with manifestation, illumination, and determination.

It is clear that this actualist vision involves a concept of finality, and in effect, the Swedenborgian system is fundamentally teleological. As a result, we can establish a consecutive series with the categories of determination, actualism, and finality: beings are determined in order to bring their being (which is a collective of their determinations) into action, to be useful; and their actions manifest an end in the totality of reality, the attainment of a goal: uses are the very ends of creation. This is true because a reality that makes all its potentialities appear would be the maximum image and representation of Divinity itself. Uses are in fact the ends of creation, and use, when developed in actions, serves as a receptacle for the divine presence, and in same measure, of reintegration in God himself. All this results in an ontological activism on all levels: in the divine, in the natural, in the human.

We will try to summarize all the important conclusions that can be reached from this. Firstly, all these categories (or we could say all these determinations) have an operative and active correlation (use). Thus, there is nothing abstract in Swedenborg; everything marches and progresses toward form and manifestation (that is, toward action). Secondly, the movement of reality (the human and natural spheres) leads to the actualization of the inherent potential of those spheres. Stated in Swedenborgian terms, the degrees of reality unfold and are manifested in use (acts, effects, action), which is the ultimate fulfillment of those degrees. In the case of biblical exegesis (of vital importance for Swedenborg), the presence of action assumes the literal sense of biblical interpretation. In turn, all this ontological actualism implies an organicism, vitalism, and teologism on the part of Swedenborg's system. The progression in the opening of the degrees means the successive attainment of the intrinsic potential of reality. However, in reference to humans it has a special transcendence and meaning: the capacity of human beings to be open to their ontological possibilities, that is, the fulfillment of degrees, is a way of thinking about humans as open beings, as *ex-isting* (from the Latin root of the word, "standing out"). Regarding *ex-isting*, humans in and of themselves are not anything; they are pure possibility and therefore, in some ways, can be anything. Humans can open themselves to the three natural degrees and to the three degrees of the spiritual world. Therefore, the human is a being from top to bottom, a being whose pure possibility in its "nothingness" opens itself up to everything. When everything is present in the openness that is the human being, it means that the person is becoming actualized and attaining his or her open degrees. In Swedenborgian language, the person's mind increases or, as Henry Corbin states, a process of intensification of forms arises.

The ontology of intensification of forms consists of the possibility that humans acquire a plurality of metaphysical forms to the degree in which they ascend in their spiritual fulfillment. This concept—comparable to so many mystical, Neoplatonic, and gnostic systems—makes humans beings open *(aperiuntur)* to the acquisition of gradually superior ontological states. To the degree in which one ascends *(elevatio mentis)* the scale of the degrees, the soul becomes part of this degree or form, that is, the means of being and the means of comprehending coincide. We can then deduce that for Swedenborg the principle of individuation lies in the form. Human beings' condition of openness facilitates the installation of different metaphysical forms, that is, being occurs in humans according to a certain phenomenology. Thus we have called the intensification of forms a mystical existentialism, because it assumes that humans do not possess a fixed essence beforehand, but that the being of humans continues to be formed during their existence, during living, which is a continual acquisition of forms. It is as if the Understanding Agent (*dator formarum* in the era of medieval philosophy) were informing humans not from a purely cognitive point of view, but rather an integrative, experiential, and existential one. Let us make note that in Swedenborg's case, the primary factor in the process of acquisition of forms is love rather than the more intellectual powers, which gives a special tenor to Swedenborg's system. Whoever loves more, is more; in this Swedenborg clearly distinguishes himself from other theosophic currents, since for him love is specifically what makes humans different (we stress again the importance of pietism in Swedenborg's formation). Finally, anthropology concludes in angelology; this means that the final form of human beings is the angel.[10]

A summary of Swedenborg's anthropology—anthropology that leads into an angelology—could be: humanity is not something given, but rather something that must be continually obtained. We are, then, in the presence of a process of personalization. Humans are (or they become) like ontological forms that are opened and assimilate. Humans are more human the more they assimilate the forms that are precisely what makes them more human: love and wisdom, with preference always on love. When Swedenborg refers human qualities to God, he is not anthropomorphizing divinity, but rather, above all, he is affirming that humans are more human the more they are compared to God, the human archetype. Thus, in Swedenborg there is a humanism, but one that is dynamic and existential: humanity is something that humans need to conquer, and ultimately their humanity consists of their angels. Here, as Corbin has rightly pointed out, angelology and anthropology coincide. Angels, heaven, and the church are not separated entities or superimposed on humans; they are the humans that all humans can be. For example, it could seem paradoxical that a book such as *Divine Love and Wisdom* ends with a description of the formation of the fetus (§432). But for the reader who has captured the marrow of Swedenborg's thought, there will be no such paradox. In reality there is nothing more consequential in his entire work, since the wisdom of angels regarding divine love and divine wisdom is not something that belongs only to celestial heights or esoteric depths. Rather, it embraces the entire process by which humans themselves (by virtue of their state of openness) become humans, and fulfill and achieve all their potentialities, from the embryo to the angel: the *terminus a quo* and *terminus ad quem* of the constitution, determination, and formalization of the human person.

If we can say that humans are in some ways all things (inasmuch as they make all things present), also, and for that same reason, we can affirm that all things are like the human being insofar as the human is the openness in which everything becomes present (stated in Swedenborg's words: insofar as the All—heaven, God himself—has the form of humans). This does not mean that Swedenborg anthropomorphizes or subjectivizes reality (and certainly not God), but rather, when he represents the openness of humans as the presence of all states of being, from top to bottom, that becomes the very model of original openness. The Presence makes itself present according to the ontological degree of the subject that receives it. Stated in Swedenborgian terms, the ontological degree becomes the wisdom and love that possesses each receptive subject. A subjective impression of the Presence is given to the consciousness of the receptive subject, and therefore there are a plurality of ways for the Presence to present itself, depending on the plurality of consciousness itself. Thus, there is an internalization of philosophical and religious categories in Swedenborg: the spiritual world is found where the human is found.

All this ontological development toward form and action are in a reciprocal relationship with other fundamental categories in Swedenborg. We refer to vitalism, organicism, and teleologism. It is clear that inasmuch as Swedenborg reacts against a mechanist vision of the world and of humans, life itself is the instantiation with the greatest prevalence as an internal cause of the movement of reality. In fact, the movement, the attempt, the force that impels everything toward determination and form rests in the vital element that stimulates the diverse orders of being. There is, therefore, a trend from the crystallizing phase to the phase of intelligence that imprints a direction on the development and appearance of distinct organizational entities. "Direction" here refers to meaning and purpose. The progressive order of the determinations (which is the order that moves reality from the crystallizing to the intelligence phase) comes from an impulse or influx that drives everything to its fulfillment, toward its being, toward its form. The progressive overcoming of one phase by another phase is due to that organic effort that strives toward the fullness of all reality. Thus, the graduated vision of totality obeys a step-by-step process in the achievement of ends—stated in other words, in the attainment of the manifestation that is appropriate to each being and in the attainment of the ultimate finality itself. From all this vitalism, organicism, and teleologism emerges Swedenborg's division of reality into degrees, kingdoms, orders, and phases of a process toward Love and Intelligence. This vital impulse of which we speak does not end in the natural sphere, with humans, but rather through the human it navigates toward spiritual worlds, where it continues the progression toward superior forms of Intelligence and Love, since Swedenborg's teleology is universal, thorough, and involves totality. The emergent force of the vital impulse extends from the fetus to the angel (in the synchronic or horizontal plane), from the petrographic phase to the most spiritually pure phase (according to the diachronic or vertical plane). It has its final state precisely in the emergence of all the forms and determinations of reality in the order of the constitution of ontological fullness (hence, as stated above, we find not even a hint of acosmism in our author); this ontological fullness is characterized more than anything by love, instead of any other intellectual qualification.

In this manner, Swedenborg's division of reality is rooted in concepts that unify the visionary elements of the book of Revelation and its nuptial mysticism as a symbol of fullness through love (we know the importance that Swedenborg concedes to this book by all the commentaries he dedicated to it) with Neoplatonic metaphysics represented by John Scotus Eriugena, St. Maximus the Confessor, and Nicholas of Kues, for example. To all this we could add the line of thinkers dominated by an existential passion with the drive to transcend all ontological horizons, such as Unamuno, Berdyaev, or Shestov.[11]

The classification of the phases of reality into degrees means nothing less than what we have just said. These degrees speak to us of how the forms emerge, moved by vital impulse. Each degree is another step in the ladder of higher determinations: the more something is determined, the more it has being, identity, individuality, intelligence, and love. For this reason Swedenborg places the figure of the human being as a prototype and model for all determination, since humans exemplify the possibility of attainment of all these qualifications, or in other words, the possibility of maximum determination. It should be of no surprise that for Swedenborg creation appears to be an escalation toward full humanization (something that is also common in line of thinkers to which Swedenborg belongs). From there, as we have stated, the same divine realities are humanly configured, because these are the highest attainments of determination.

The theory of degrees (or of the intensification of forms) more obviously demonstrates all those categories of which we have spoken. The theory of degrees means, first of all, that there is an order to all reality; and secondly, a progression of this order from the least to the most, from the indeterminate toward the determinate: it definitely means an ascendant line that thrusts the world toward its abundance. For Swedenborg there are two types of degrees: those of height and those of width. All beings carry inside themselves this double movement represented by the degrees of height and width. In turn, the classification of these two types of degrees in three phases is due to the general structure that Swedenborg creates, according to which, by virtue of correspondences and representations, all spheres analogically repeat the superior spheres. Thus, the degrees of height are divided into low, medium, and tall (in the image and likeness of the three heavens: lower, middle, and upper). In turn, the degrees of width can be interior, middle, and exterior. The ranking of beings is ontological and categorical, not empirical and ontic, at least among the three degrees of nature: each one of them is the ontological improvement of the preceding one, without any factual conversion of one degree into another. Humans overcome and assume the three preceding states, but once they arrive at the spiritual sphere there is a continuation in the conversion from one degree to another. Naturally, the final spiritual degree will take on all the other preceding states, so that the angelological projection of human beings carries with it the assumption of all things in God.

It is not of interest here to go into detail about Swedenborg's various theories, which are mixes of a traditional speculative vision and of the scientific discoveries of his era. What is crucial is to make clear how the theory of degrees impacts the fundamental concepts of Swedenborg's system, especially concerning the notions of determination, configuration, and finality.

The theory of degrees signifies the movement of determination itself and of the progression toward form. The degree of height indicates the external level in which a particular entity is located—its position on the vertical line that runs through all of creation, from the mineral kingdom to the last heavenly kingdom. The degree of width indicates the inward situation of that same particular entity, its advance toward its innermost nucleus. In addition, the theory of degrees shows us how the vital impulse marches toward finality, how the potentialities are actualized and configured. Thus, the theory of degrees puts all of creation in movement, opens beings to new ontological possibilities, and leads beings to their formal realization. As can also be shown, the theory of degrees and its sense of metaphysical openness serves Swedenborg as a way of explaining one of the most profound motivations that drive his system: the connection between the intelligible and the perceptible, between the spiritual and the material. At the same time, the theory of degrees becomes the inner life of all things: it is the means by which life flows and determinations are conformed. Swedenborg's theory of degrees imparts a feeling of infinity, but of an infinity that doesn't dissolve forms, but rather creates them; of an infinity that is not abstract, but rather adds material as it materializes; of an infinity that is, then, determination.

2

THE ROLE OF THE SUBJECT
IN SWEDENBORG

In Swedenborg there is a category that plays a special role and that we consider a type of guiding principle for our reflections: we refer to the category of the subject. In effect, when we deeply analyze and see the inner meaning of his work, we realize that the priority of the subject is a constant element in Swedenborg's totalizing vision. Thus for Swedenborg the subject (i.e., the human being, the person) is an element that takes priority in reality. The ontological claim of the human being is contrasted against the instantiations that can annul or dissolve the physicality of this human subject. We can affirm that Swedenborg's philosophy is a philosophy of subjectivity, a philosophy that reclaims subjectivity as a qualitative factor of reality. We believe that the causes of this phenomenon are, among other things, the following: in the face of the growing rise of a science that offers a purely quantitative image of the world, in which qualitative substance hardly, if at all, has a specific role to play, Swedenborg responds with an impulse to restore the subject and its motivations. In short, Swedenborg defends the person in an environment that tends precisely toward depersonalization. For this reason we believe that the priority of the subject is a hermeneutical key for penetrating the thought of the wise Swede, and that it explains many of the other philosophical, theological, and symbolic themes of our author.

If we place the progressive dissolution of the category of the subject together with the likewise progressive disappearance of this same category in the scientific sphere, we would have another reason for the presence of the personalizing factor in Swedenborg. The importance of the subject means not wanting to eliminate the specifically personal and human element of the scientific operation and sphere. It means, thus, to involve the subject in science vitally and existentially.[1] It would involve the search for affinity (in Swedenborgian language: correspondence) between consciousness and the world, between the *res extensa* (corporeal substance) and the *res cogitans* (mental substance).[2] It would involve the recognition of the subject in the external realm, and for him this would not be devoid of meaning.[3] It would mean that consciousness is not lost in the impersonality of a world and of a science that are channeled toward the purely quantitative. Thus the recognition of subjectivity is interwoven with ontological determination, and, to be more precise, with determination as personalization.[4] To overlap subjectivity with the very structure of external reality assumes one is making that external reality a qualitative and significant factor; it assumes, in short, that it will be adapted and confirmed in light of the decisions and impulses of consciousness, thus establishing a vision in which the inner and outer spheres are not foreign to each other. Hence the existential character of Swedenborg, hence also the defense of the ontological dimension of the subject, except that all this finds itself expressed in the peculiar templates of Swedenborg's language.

It is well understood that Swedenborg doesn't try to devalue science. Swedenborg was one of the great scientists of his era. He studied humanities in Uppsala and expanded his studies in Holland, France, Italy, and England, where he devoted himself to the reading of Newton. He designed a submarine, a system of floodgates, and a helicopter, and collaborated with the Swedish inventor Christopher Polhem. Swedenborg possessed profound knowledge of the movement of the Earth and the planets, of algebra, and differential and integral calculus, as well as geology, paleontology, and anatomy. One could also consider him the founder of crystallography in the modern sense. His cosmological theory of the origin of the universe was a forerunner to those of Buffon, Kant, and Laplace. Given this scientific grounding, his system does not lead to any kind of acosmism or negation of exterior reality. Swedenborg's intention lies in locating the subject and its contents within the order provided by science and in the order of reality itself, thus averting the alienation or dissolving of the subject and its contents in a supposed reified and quantified objectification of reality.[5]

This fact is what leads us to consider Swedenborg as a philosopher who reinstates the precedence of the subject as a qualitative and personal element of reality as a whole, to approach the ideas and categories of his system within the parameters of the subject, and to connect the Swedish thinker with the line of thinkers that are distinguished by the recognition and recovery of the qualitative—as opposed to the purely quantitative and objective—substance of the subject.

Let us examine some ways in which all this is shown in Swedenborg's writings.

For Swedenborg, the maximum perfection given to human beings consists of the full realization of all their possibilities. But this pleromatic realization transforms humans into angels; Swedenborg's anthropology concludes in angelology. Does this not mean that humans have to stop being themselves in order to fulfill their essence? Does this not contradict what we stated earlier? No, if we keep in mind that the angel is nothing more than an ontologically realized human (the form of the angel is human); no, if we keep in mind that God himself is human, that is, model and archetype for the very humanity of humans, hypostatically made explicit in Christ; no, if, ultimately, heaven itself—the pleroma—is a human (the symbol of Macranthropos).

This is illustrated in several places in Swedenborg's writings:

> God is the essential person. Throughout all the heavens, the only concept of God is a concept of a person. The reason is that heaven, overall and regionally, is in a kind of human form, and Divinity among the angels is what makes heaven. Further, thinking proceeds in keeping with heaven's form, so it is not possible for angels to think about God in any other way. . . . It is because God is a person that all angels and spirits are perfectly formed people. (*Divine Love and Wisdom* §11)

> Since God is a person, the whole angelic heaven, taken as a single unit, presents itself as a single person. It is divided into regions and districts according to our human members, organs, and viscera. (*Divine Love and Wisdom* §288)

The universal human, and correspondence with it, have already been defined. The universal human is the whole of heaven, which is a composite likeness and image of the Lord. The Lord's divine nature corresponds to the heavenly and spiritual attributes there ... Through heaven or the universal human, then, the Lord's divine nature corresponds with a human being and with all the parts that make up a human being. (*Secrets of Heaven* §3883)

Here we have a reflection of the pristine and universal idea of Macranthropos or the archetypal human as constituent of the pleroma or spiritual world. When it is said that God has human form, we do not fall into a simplistic anthropocentrism, but rather we affirm the following: God (and the spiritual world) is not ineffable or a bottomless abyss; humans participate in its essential configuration and determination to the degree that humans are a reflection of the primordial Human. Furthermore, Swedenborg reveals to us a completely internalized conception of the spiritual world, inasmuch as the form of God is the form of heaven and the form of thought. That is: God is in every thought of every human being of every heaven (of his own heaven, of his own interiority). All this means that the spiritual fulfillment of humans beings is based on the fulfillment of their own humanity, in being fully human.

We find ourselves before a mystical or ontological existentialism, where the will of the human being inclines toward the realization of the Human Form that is Love (in imitation of the Supreme Form that is God).

In Swedenborg's words:

There is not a single individual or angel so like another that there is no difference. Love is what makes the difference, each individual being her or his own love. (*Divine Love and Wisdom* §368)

All the people in that world are forms of their love. (*Divine Love and Wisdom* §369)

We can see from this that love—and from love, our volition, and from volition, our hearts—is constantly striving toward the human form. (*Divine Love and Wisdom* §400)

In Swedenborg everything gravitates toward form, toward configuration. There is nothing in him that refers us to monism or any other type of annulling mysticism, nor is there any bottomless and indeterminate abyss. On the contrary, the ontological fullness of his spirituality is prone to qualification, determination, and form. Therefore, Swedenborg's thought is essentially representative, that is, it ends up as an ontology of the concrete image and not of the abstract concept. The idea of human beings' propensity toward existence, toward taking form, makes Swedenborg's system a type of mystical existentialism in which conceptual categories such as essence and existence tend to be replaced by the more representative categories of love and wisdom. "In the Divine-Human One, reality and its manifestation are both distinguishable and united. . . . They are distinguishably one like love and wisdom. Further, love is reality and wisdom is its manifestation. . . . The reason reality is not reality unless it is manifested is that before that happens it has no form" (*Divine Love and Wisdom* §§14–15).

Swedenborg returns to the old notion of Macranthropos, of the primordial and archetypal human, a figure that since the Avestan Gayomard or the Vedic Prajapati has been appearing with a logical metamorphosis through all the traditional doctrines, as much in the West as in the East. Romanticism, influenced by Swedenborg, adopted this same theme of the primordial human. The figure of the Macranthropos is complex and multifaceted. We will limit ourselves for now by saying that for Swedenborg the Great Human (which is heaven itself, the pleroma) could be equivalent to the concept of Logos, like the idea of the human being as it appears in Philo of Alexandria. In this sense, to say that heaven is the Great Human is like saying that Logos is the Logos that corresponds to humans, that the human is all the more human as it resembles or assimilates the Logos; that, all in all, the Logos that corresponds to the human is Logos itself.[6]

And if "the spiritual world is right where we are" (*Divine Love and Wisdom* §92), hell will consist of not being able to be human, in not wholly developing all the spiritual possibilities of the human being. Humans are heaven or hell to the degree in which they open or close themselves to the presence of the divine light. If humans open their inner selves to receive this presence, they phenomenalize the light;

the Presence comes over the human soul, and thus the human becomes truth, or wisdom, or heaven. The opposite occurs when humans close themselves to the possibility of receiving meaning, and then the human becomes hell.

Continuing with our exposition of the categories common to Swedenborg and to mystical-representative thought (as related to the theme of subject), the concept of correspondence is essential for this type of conception. It is not necessary to explain the multiple variations in which we can find the idea of correspondence: spirit/matter, intelligible/material, superior/inferior, model/image, etc. But we particularly want to focus on one variety of the ideas about correspondence. We refer to the *melosias,* the exhaustive enumerations of the concrete correspondences of the human with its model in the higher sphere, particularly with the Great Human. As can be shown, we are dealing with another traditional image that has a special interest for the subject; in fact, the *melosia* denotes a treatment based in the ontological constitution of the subject, but only in mythic and representative form. In effect, the profound meaning of the category of *melosia* consists of showing the intelligible component of each human part or element; that is, the *melosia* reveals the presence of the sacred in humans and connects humans with their model. By means of *melosia* the subject becomes a representation and receptacle of the transcendent sphere, whereupon the transcendent sets itself up as subject and meaning is imbued in the human subject itself by virtue of its condition as an image or reflection.

This is a constant theme in Swedenborg, especially in *Secrets of Heaven.* This citation serves as an example: "The whole of heaven has been formed to correspond with the Lord and his divine humanity. Human beings have been formed to correspond in absolutely every particular with heaven, and through heaven with the Lord. . . . That explains why it is said several times in preceding sections describing heaven and communities of angels that they belonged to some region of the body, like that of the head, chest, abdomen, or some part or organ lodging there; the reason is the above-mentioned correspondence" (*Secrets of Heaven* §3624–5).

The possibility of establishing *melosia* or correspondences between our world and the divine world is based on the fact that in God we find all the corporal elements that are in humans—that is, Divinity is configured with determinations that, in turn, ontologically determine the human:

> Because if God is a person, he has a body and everything that having a body entails. So he has a face, torso, abdomen, upper legs, and lower legs, since without these he would not be a person. Since he has these components, he also has eyes, ears, nose, mouth, and tongue. He also has what we find within a person, such as a heart and lungs and the things that depend on them, all of which, taken together, make us human. We are created with these many components, and if we consider them in their interconnections, they are beyond counting. In the Divine-Human One, though, they are infinite. Nothing is lacking, so he has an infinite completeness. We can make this comparison of the uncreated Person, who is God, with us who are created, because that God is a person. It is because of [his being a person] that we earthly beings are said to have been created in his image and in his likeness (Genesis 1:26, 27). (*Divine Love and Wisdom* §18)

This is no simplistic anthropocentrism, but rather it follows a very profound motivation. The unknowability of God is resolved by means of a series of mediations or theophanies that show the presence of Divinity in all orders of reality and, through *melosia*, in the human being. Thus, the apophatism is overcome by an action in which God is stated, determined, and manifested through mediations *(receptacula)*; the *melosias* fulfill, then, this ontological and theophanic role in the particular case of humans. "Then consider that the Lord cannot make himself manifest to any angel or to us as he really is and as he is in his sun. This is why he makes himself manifest by means of things that can be accepted" (*Divine Love and Wisdom* §299).

There is a matter we need to discuss here concerning the theory of correspondences. We refer to Swedenborg's influence on Romanticism, an influence that in our judgment is based in part on the popularization—thanks to the rapid diffusion of Swedenborg's books—of the old theory of correspondences among Romantics. But why this theory in particular? To what profound cause is its ascendancy due? The symbolic correspondence between the world above and the world below is what impedes the separation between both worlds, while it also allows the connection of our sphere with the transcendent. This connection is rooted in the spiritual interpretation of the symbols that constitute our reality. That is, the discovery of the spiritual dimension of the world below and its elevation to the transcendent world is accomplished by the ontology of representations and correspondences. Thus the *jorismós,* the break between the material and the spiritual, the intelligible and the material, is covered over. Thus, the religious Romantic consciousness, which itself is split between the I and the not-I, discovered in Swedenborg's correspondences a way of overcoming that tragically lived duality. Stated in the words of Jean-Marc Tisserant: "The theory of correspondences was the legacy of Swedenborg for the innumerable masses that painfully lived the disparity of heaven and earth, of dream and reality, to all who, in the spheres of poetry and of mysticism, despaired of reducing heavy matter to a pure mercurial substance."[7] In this way we summarize the existential character of Swedenborg's thought, in that his assumptions respond to necessities vividly proposed from his radical existentialism.

All the instantiations that phenomenological analysis confirms in Swedenborg are intertwined and interconnected. Therefore, any of them connects us with a notional and spiritual complex of similar characteristics. For instance, the idea of syzygy is another constant in Swedenborg's work in relation to the theme of subject. For the Scandinavian philosopher all ontological determinations articulate in dichotomies, in such a way that celestial marriages (i.e., syzygies) are established among the polar elements. Accordingly, there is a conjugal union between Good and Truth, Thought and Will, Creator and Creature, etc., which makes Swedenborg's entire system express itself to us as a personalized and personalizing conception of reality. In this way it acquires its ontological fullness, its *coincidentia oppositorum,* in terms of nuptial realization. "It is also an item of angelic wisdom that that perfection of the created universe comes from a resemblance in regard to levels between the inclusive forms and their particular constituents, or between the largest and smallest things. This means that each thing sees the other as a kindred with which it can unite in its whole function and with which it can realize its whole purpose in actual results" (*Divine Love and Wisdom* §227). The universal correspondence among all things facilitates a fulfillment of the syzygy also among all things.

In other words, each thing has the possibility of establishing a syzygy with its semblance or correspondent.

The category of *connubio* (marriage) is correlative of that of the *conjuctivus* (the joining together of tangible reality) since the conjunction of all reality with its archetype or celestial part is seen as the ontological fulfillment of everything real. Here one can cite some representative passages from Swedenborg:

> The grand purpose, or the purpose of all elements of creation, is an eternal union of the Creator with the created universe. (*Divine Love and Wisdom* §170)

> In support of this I may include here a portrayal of the correspondence of volition and discernment with the heart and the lungs . . . In this way they portrayed the union of the heart and the lungs and at the same time their correspondence with volition's love and discernment's wisdom. They call this correspondence and union a "heavenly marriage." (*Divine Love and Wisdom* §376)

> Love or volition prepares a home or bridal chamber for its spouse-to-be, wisdom or discernment. In the created universe and in every detail of it there is a marriage between what is good and what is true. (*Divine Love and Wisdom* §402)

Naturally, this gives us an idea of the importance of the theme of marriage or conjugal union for Swedenborg (ultimately, it is always about issues that affect the human subject). Correspondences are established among all spheres of existence, between the highest (the angelic world, heaven) and the lowest (the human body, which in this way forms a type of microcosm). The *conjugium caeleste* (heavenly marriage) is a fundamental category for Swedenborg, and so with it there is a desire to express the fact that ontological fullness establishes itself in terms of love. Consequently, and as we mentioned earlier, it is expressed in personalized and personalizing terms, and the syzygy is universal. One could relate Swedenborg's *conjugium caeleste* with the *misterion conjuctionis* (resolution of conflict between poles) of alchemy, the *hierogamos* (gods and goddesses uniting in marriage), or the marriage of Christ and the Church. Undoubtedly, the nuptial symbolism of our author is of biblical origin.[8]

The theme of heavenly nuptials in Swedenborg, as with the subsumption of everything real under the marital categories of Wisdom and Love, has a profound meaning. First of all, we can see the utilization of a sexualized sense of spiritual reality that finds its origins, at least, in the biblical Song of Solomon. Secondly, all orders of reality participate in this sexualized spirituality, which means that all of reality is incorporated into the dialectic of unifying love. In turn, this implies that one finds the intellectual categories of being together with the categories of volition, love, and affectivity (which have higher ontological importance). Thirdly, with the argument of heavenly nuptials, Swedenborg raises again the old theme of syzygy, that is, of the union of the soul with its celestial correspondence: that part through which, by means of pairing through marriage, we obtain our true self. And finally, we emphasize again the importance of the subject and its activity, the preponderant role it adopts throughout all of Swedenborg's writings.

All the problematic issues raised in Swedenborg's texts, which are prolifically addressed in *De Deliciae Sapientiae De Amore Conjugali (Marriage Love)*, are about the passionate search for our true selves by means of a symbolic matrimonial link. Here Swedenborg connects with the tradition that contemplates the spiritual realization that humans are a passionate integration of lover and loved, of gentleman and lady. At the same time, Swedenborg reintroduces this theme into Romanticism, creating a unifying bridge between the older tradition and the new forms of spirituality that emerge with Romantics. Swedenborg inscribes himself in the tradition that considers marriage to be the realization in fullness of humans (and all of reality). It thus connects with the book of Revelation, which also conceives of the pleromatic moment in terms of marriage.[9] Through union with their archetype and through conjugal love (symbol and image of all conjunction), humans and all of creation are restored to fullness. Here we have the ultimate meaning of Swedenborg's thought. This conception departs from the Johannine corpus and continues in the Patristics and John Scotus Eriugena; we believe, as we have already stated, that it has an illustrious representative in Swedenborg, and that after his time the chain continues in Oetinger, Schelling, Franz Xaver von Baader, and the Russian spiritualists. The lineage of Origen, Gregory of Nyssa, and John Scotus Eriugena is effectively present in the Swede's system: creation is integrated in its fullness through the action of human beings, who are in turn integrated into that same fullness because they are attracted by the logophanic mediation of Christ. In summary, what Swedenborg does is to discover the spiritual value of all material things.

We have expounded a series of philosophical, theological, and symbolic themes that share the same issue: the prevalent position given to the subject. Through diverse paths Swedenborg always concludes by stressing the constituent factors of the human subject. Person and personalization are not anecdotal or isolated elements in Swedenborg's system: they are its backbone. The ontological and qualitative recognition of the subject presents itself to us as a type of hermeneutical key that makes many facets of Swedenborg comprehensible for us, facets that, without that key, could remain misunderstood or unintelligible.

One last consideration remains: the endless theme of Macranthropos and its relationship to the subject. We refer to the interpretation that C. G. Jung gives of the alchemistic notion of *homo totus*. For Jung the objective and goal of alchemistic action is the achievement of a *homo totus,* that is, of an integrated human being, a human being that has realized a totality of the self. It is not necessary to belabor the point in order to establish an equivalence between the concept of *homo totus* and Swedenborg's *homo maximus,* similar not only in name, but also in content, since it is legitimate to see in the Great Human of Swedenborg the collective sense of human totality as the integrated realization of human essence. At that time, Jung himself interpreted the distinct mythical figures of the archetypical human (Gayomard, Purusa, the gnostic Anthropos, Metatron, etc.) as the mythic origin of humanity and at the same time as the possibility on the part of the concrete human being to acquire the characteristic that defines the archetypical human: the totality of human perfection. Alchemical activity and speculation center around the attainment of this. In both cases, the alchemistic *homo totus* or the *homo maximus* would be projections aimed at expressing the potential fullness of human beings. All this leads us to think that it would be very fruitful to apply more of Swedenborg's categories to Jungian analysis.[10]

3

HERMENEUTICS AND INNER EXPERIENCE

Of the many components of Swedenborg's work that make it comparable (in some measure) to the great products of gnostic religiosity, we have to emphasize above all the specific role of Swedenborg's spiritual hermeneutics. These hermeneutics are in solidarity with a prophetic philosophy, with a representative ontology, that depends, ultimately, on its belonging to a revealed Book and to the necessity of internalizing the meaning of that Book.[1] Let us state from the outset that hermeneutics in Swedenborg are not an isolated or circumstantial fact. On the contrary, they form one of the pillars of his thought and of his own ecstatic experience, to such an extent that we cannot separate his spiritual hermeneutics from his ontology or visionary life, those spheres being combined in a robust and unitary conception. In all of gnosticism there are three basic motivations: one is of substantial character, that is, it attempts to answer the question of the ontological constitution of reality; another is salvific, that is, it entails a soteriological interest that tries to explain the transcendental dimension of the human being; the third motivation is of exegetical character, and it is what moves gnostic experience and speculation, given their dependence on a revealed Book.[2] So we can say that, to a certain point, even the substantial and salvific spheres are conditioned by the hermeneutical sphere being put into practice. In this sense we consider that gnosticism—as Henri-Charles Puech already affirmed—is fundamentally an exegesis. It also follows, and this supports our idea, that gnostics born in the bosom of other religions of the Book are distinguished by their special exegetical tenor. In effect, belonging to a religious sphere determined by the fact of a sacred text generates some specific hermeneutics— we will call them spiritual hermeneutics—that condition the appearance of gnostic and other similar currents.[3] Valentinism, kabbalah, or Ismailism have as a common factor their reference to a revealed text. At the same time, they share a similar attitude toward that text: spiritual access to hidden meaning under scriptural symbols. Here hermeneutics and mysticism coincide, since to interpret the symbolic language of the Book means to examine and experience these same symbols internally. Thus a theosophy of the Word emerges, a prophetic philosophy, a mysticism in which the symbols of the Book and the symbols of the soul affect, exchange, and identify with each other. So the hidden sense of the Book that the interpreter experiences through the interpretation is his transcendental part, *his* angel, *his* meaning.

Swedenborg is a thinker who completely shares all these exegetical-spiritual experiences. In fact, we have to consider Swedenborg a champion of spiritual hermeneutics; we can even say that in certain respects his philosophical-theological work is nothing other than biblical commentary, an interpretation of the spiritual sense of the Bible. His exegesis is a corollary or an extrapolation to the scriptural world of the purpose behind all his thought: to seek out and discover the innermost part of reality. What Swedenborg seeks through his visions is to find the celestial meaning—the angel—of the words of the revealed text and its corresponding meaning in the transcendental world. Or better yet, his visions themselves are the manifestation of a meaning hidden beneath a layer of symbols. We believe that Swedenborg's entire philosophical-theological system depends, in large part, on spiritual hermeneutics—just as, for example, all kabbalistic speculation depends on spiritual exegesis. This is just like saying that Swedenborg's philosophical-theological system depends on the inner experience of the apprehension and assimilation of meaning (hence the existential dimension of all spiritual hermeneutics). In fact, we can affirm that Swedenborg's exegetical work is a grandiose midrash (as is the case in kabbalah). By this we are not proposing that Swedenborg has a historical dependency on the kabbalah or on midrashic Hebrew literature. By calling Swedenborg's implemented interpretations midrashism, we mean he has an identical phenomenology of interpretation in the spiritual sense; a phenomenology that is based on themes, principles, and experiences equally common to midrashic literature, to the kabbalah, or to the Scandinavian thinker.[4] The comparative study of kabbalistic exegesis and Swedenborg's exegesis makes it possible for both to be called midrashic (likewise, one could say the same about Shiite exegesis). The midrashic character is determined by the following fundamentals: foremost, obviously, by our author's membership in the religious sphere of the revealed Book. But naturally this is not something that in itself characterizes a thinker or a current such as spiritual hermeneutics. For that, one needs a special attitude in the presence of that revealed Book, an attitude that stems from the identification between substantial explanation, salvific path, and exegesis, translating all this into a philosophy of language in which the word has the meaning, and it gives meaning to the interpreter. This attitude is what is manifested in the kabbalah, and Swedenborg, and all that we call midrashic. As stated earlier, the purpose of Swedenborg's theological work is to serve as an interpretation of the Bible. Through his spiritual interpretation, he reveals the supersensible realities and their relation to the life of the soul (the internalized inner self). In order to accomplish this he implements a whole series of images and experiences that account for the triple function that motivates the gnostic consciousness. Accordingly, we begin to see in Swedenborg ideas and themes such as dreams, visions, angels, supersensory regions, and so on—always referring to the question of the hidden sense of the sacred text. In reality, all these examples that we have enumerated, and many more, are nothing more than specifications and revelations of meaning. They are symbols through which the hidden meaning is expressed and made statable.

The meanings of Scripture are and correspond to the transcendental states of being. Thus, to interpret Scripture is to discover the spiritual or celestial content that underlies the text, to show the celestial or spiritual dimension of a text. It is a matter of elevating the terrestrial, literal, or corporal dimension, so that the other, transcendental dimension appears:

When I asked them whether they realized that there was a spiritual meaning in every detail of the Word, though, and that this is the meaning the Word has in heaven, they said at first they did not realize this. However, later they said they would ask, and when they did they were told that there was in the details of the Word a spiritual meaning that was as different from the literal meaning as the spiritual is from the earthly. They were also told that no character named in the Word is so named in heaven, but that some spiritual reality is understood in place of the character . . . When they read it they saw quite clearly that there was no mention of Peter there but of "truth, inspired by good intent, from the Lord" instead. (*Revelation Unveiled* §768)

If we could define Swedenborg's hermeneutics, we would say that for the wise Swede the meaning of the Bible refers to its spiritual and celestial sense. "The Word does in fact have a literal meaning and a spiritual meaning. The literal meaning consists of the kind of things that are in our world, while the spiritual meaning consists of the kinds of things that are in heaven; and since the union of heaven with our world is maintained by correspondences, we have been given a Word in which the details correspond, even down to the last jot" (*Heaven and Hell* §114; see also *True Christianity* §23).

From here proceeds an entire exegetical movement, one intended to clarify the spiritual and celestial meanings trapped inside the appearance of the words. But this exegetical apparatus is not based on categories or abstract concepts; rather, it will be expressed in terms of ecstatic experience and of personal instantiations. This is one of the reasons why angelology is a fundamental theme in Swedenborg. In all celestial visions a guide is necessary to direct and indicate the way for the seer, while at the same time this champion needs also to be the *angelus interpres*, that is, the figure that makes the hidden sense of the Book clear.[5]

We stated that Swedenborg's theological-exegetical work is a midrashic development of the Bible. We already know that the word midrash is taken here not in the strictly technical sense, but rather as a commentary that flows from reflection on and internalization of a sacred text. In this regard, the literatures of the Heichalot and of the kabbalah are midrashim of the Torah, that is, mystical interpretations of texts and

Bible passages. More specifically, given the visionary character of those midrashim, we could speak of midrashic *pesher* (interpretation) as the most adequate to define this type of experience.[6] Swedenborg inserts himself in this resultant tradition of spiritual exegesis of symbolic text represented in the Book. This exegesis attempts to attain the deep meaning that the words or the apparent meaning reveal.

But Swedenborg does not disdain the literal or natural sense; rather, this sense corresponds with the more profound or superior senses, of which the literal significance is their epiphany *in suo pleno et in sua potentia*. Tying this idea to Swedenborg's ontology, the literal or natural sense would be equivalent to the use, that is, to the effective determination of all its spiritual content, explained and manifested precisely in the final state of this gradual development of the senses: only because of the presence of the literal sense can we know the preceding sense. Here we have a scriptural process of anabasis and of katabasis parallel to the similar ontological process: "Since the Word contains these three meanings by the three vertical levels and their union is through correspondence, the final meaning, the earthly one that we call the literal meaning, is not only the composite, vessel, and foundation of the deeper, corresponding meanings, it is also the Word in its fullest expression and its full power" (*Divine Love and Wisdom* §221).

The visionary journey is a journey in search of the different spheres of meaning contained in the Book; the visionary journey consists of revealing—creating epiphanies, phenomenalizing—the symbols through all of the ways they develop and unfold. Angels play a key role here, as shown in the phenomenology of the visionary narrative. The angel is the interpreter of meaning showing itself; it is meaning itself manifesting, and it is the meaning characteristic of and specific to the recipient of the vision. In summary, the angel signifies the illuminated side of the biblical word, its transcendental meaning. Consequently, the visionary experience of angels in Swedenborg is really anagogy, *ta'wil, tikkun*. That is to say, it is always a matter of redirecting the letter of the text to its celestial place, of overcoming appearances so that the epiphany of meaning can take place. It means the restoration of the profound meaning that pulsates under the scriptural symbolism. All these exegetical operations (anagogy, *ta'wil, tikkun*) respond to the experience of meaning.

The angel is meaning, epiphany, revelation, mediation, illumination: all this, but in the form of a person. The meaning that is discovered is the meaning that existentially affects the subject who is receiving the revelation; the relationship that is established between the interpreted meaning and the interpreter is a personal relationship. Therefore, the restoration *(tikkun)* of meaning and its renewal (anagogy, *ta'wil)* mean at the same time the restoration and renewal of the interpreter him- or herself. The visionary journey through the celestial realms is, then, the journey of the interpreter though the phases of meaning, which are continually revealed in the ecstatic journey. That interpreter, that companion angel, and that revealed meaning coincide: it is all the operation of Swedenborg's spiritual hermeneutics. The spiritual hermeneutics practiced and lived by our author consist of modes and characteristics common to traditional exegesis of cultures of the Book: midrash, *pesher, ta'wil, tikkun,* anagogy. This, then, is the perspective from which we must contemplate Swedenborg and his work.

The intimate union between visionary experience and hermeneutics is thus understood. Swedenborg's vision brings the biblical account to fulfillment: he experiences the spirituality of the revealed text and thereby actualizes it symbolically. Swedenborg places himself at the center of biblical prophecy because he internally accepts responsibility for that received word.[7] Therefore, he does not write a new Book. His revelation is Revelation itself, except that it is lived through him and interpreted through spiritual hermeneutics. Consequently, what is most essential in Swedenborg is his hermeneutics, which are nothing more than his own visionary experience. Hermeneutics and inner experience are correlative terms. A certain type of experience corresponds to a certain type of hermeneutics. In Swedenborg's case, for each spiritual and prophetic experience in the Bible there are corresponding hermeneutics of the spiritual sense. Inasmuch as he is the receiver of the revelation, he fulfills it and it becomes his revelation.

Swedenborg's spiritual hermeneutics are inseparable from his conception of the correspondences between the archetypal world and the material world: each passage in the text has its correspondence in the celestial or spiritual sphere. Thus, to interpret the words of a passage is to put it in relation to its celestial correspondence (to elevate it), which results in the hermeneutical key for that passage. Can we then say that the question of meaning depends on the question of the angel? Swedenborg would certainly maintain so.

We will proceed now to briefly enumerate some of the affinities between Swedenborg and the traditions of spiritual hermeneutics. First of all, there is the category of Scripture as a basis of reality, as an ontological mediation between the higher and the lower, and as a form of revelation of the superior in the inferior. Secondly, there is the stratification of the Book into layers of meaning, from the most superficial or literal to the most hidden and profound, which is accessible only through the spiritual internalizing of the meaning itself. In this way hermeneutics becomes mysticism or spiritual adventure, since each sphere of meaning coincides with an ontological sphere and with a sphere of the soul. Thus for Swedenborg the biblical meaning is extrapolated to the different cosmic spheres: the literal sense corresponds to the inferior heaven, the spiritual to the middle, and the celestial to the supreme heaven. The phenomenological relationships that can be established between Swedenborg and other spiritual hermeneutics are constructed around the meaning that the Book establishes: the angel, which is the epiphany of meaning, meaning itself, and the hermeneutics of meaning. As the meaning progresses step by step through the ontological spheres, reality itself progresses incrementally in a hierarchy of ontological spheres, and to each sphere there is a corresponding meaning or angel (and, consequently, a hermeneutical sphere).[8] This ontological, angelogical, and hermeneutical hierarchy forms a system of correspondences through which all spheres of reality find themselves connected—or, more succinctly, the superior sphere (angel, spiritual meaning, heaven) connects with the inferior sphere (humans, inner meaning, earth).

The correlation of which we speak shows us how, for spiritual hermeneutics, the ontological constitution of reality is a subsidiary of a series of spiritual instantiations that form, through a catoptrical system, the possibility of meaning and meaning itself. The Logos is manifested as the Book; the Book as mediation and manifestation is the angel; the angel, as scripture, is meaning, transcendent meaning that is made immanent. The stratification and plurality of signifiers in turn stratifies all of reality, and to each sphere of reality there is a corresponding angel or a meaning, structured according to the guidelines of the Book. All this forms a network of correspondences through which reality becomes unified depending on the Book, the angel, the meaning. We enter the world's framework of meaning by undertaking and internalizing the Book and the angel—that is, by means of the spiritual hermeneutics of meaning.

We have approached Swedenborg through the category of hermeneutics in an attempt to show the similarity that can be established between Swedenborg's exegesis and others of the same type. Phenomenological analysis and the comparative method reveal this agreement of structures, which make it possible to place Swedenborg in the same spiritual affiliation as other exegetes. We have taken this approach because in one way or another we consider spiritual hermeneutics to be the paradigm of a certain religious consciousness.

In this way Swedenborg's system is coherent, and its elements interact with each other in such a way that one cannot address a single issue or category in this system without referencing the other issues and categories. This occurs also with biblical exegesis, which as we have seen is found in close correlation with internalization. To interpret consists, in fact, in internalizing spiritual content, in obtaining a fusion of vital horizons (and these instantiations refer in turn to the instantiations of personalization, subject, etc.). A clear example of this union between hermeneutics and internalization is found in the characteristic exegesis that Swedenborg performs on the biblical Hexameron (six days of creation). In effect, our author makes an absolutely internalized interpretation of the Creation narrative: the six days represent processes and states of human consciousness that advance toward the spiritual regeneration of human beings. See, for example, *Secrets of Heaven* §4: "The inner sense of the first chapter of Genesis deals in general with the process that creates us anew—that is to say, with regeneration" and *Secrets of Heaven* §6: "The six days or time periods, meaning so many consecutive stages in a person's regeneration, are these . . ." This theme is developed in detail throughout *Secrets of Heaven* §§1–66. In Swedenborg an authentic "exegetical acceleration" is given, as Jacques Cazeaux says of Philo of Alexandria: that is, a continual recurrence of biblical quotes is given to explain the passage in question. One could say this is the same as reciting the Haggadic adagio, "In the Torah there is no before and after."

We do not believe that there is any precedent for this totally anthropological, personalizing, and internalizing exegesis. All the passages of the Creation narrative, in their internal sense, refer to stages of advancement of the soul in its progress toward conversion. This is, we repeat, the highest level of spiritualization that can be performed in a hermeneutical operation on a biblical text. One can rightly compare Swedenborg's exegesis with the inner castles of Saint Teresa of Avila, since, according to Swedenborg's explanation, the six days of creation would be effectively equivalent to the six dwellings (degrees, stages) of the soul in its journey to perfection.[9] Accordingly, we see how Swedenborg converts outer realities (in this case, a biblical narrative) into internal realities, as everything external is translated into movements of consciousness. In other words, the same categories of externality insert themselves in the process of creating the person (that is, these same categories are personalized). In short, for Swedenborg the creation of the world is, fundamentally, the creation of the inner world or creation of the spiritual human being.

4

INTERNAL TIME AND SPACE

Space does not exist in the spiritual world. Instead, distance and presence there are appearances that depend on likeness or dissimilarity of desire. (*Divine Providence* §33)

Time is simply an appearance that depends on the emotional state that gives rise to our thoughts. (*Divine Providence* §49)

There is a profound sense of the role of celestial space and time in Swedenborg. Since in the material world human beings depend on and are conditioned by time and space, in a state of fullness such as heaven time and space are dependent on humans, and thus they become determinations of consciousness. In fact, what Swedenborg wants to express is the desire to free ourselves from the burden of material conditioning, from that which obstructs us and opposes our free spontaneity. In a situation where the spiritual predominates it is the human subject that prevails over the material, that then ceases to oppose consciousness in order to be transformed into a manifestation and projection of the movements of consciousness. We would say, then, that in the spiritual experience revealed in Swedenborg's works, consciousness produces its own temporality and its own spatiality. These two factors thus become the contents of consciousness itself. What appears is its innermost meaning, and the assumption of that meaning signifies that the consciousness has internalized that same innermost meaning. Spiritual predominance means spontaneity of consciousness—space and time are not conditions of possibility, but rather inwardness itself is the condition of possibility. We can apply these words of Jean Brun to Swedenborg: "The beating of the heart implies not only the consciousness of otherness, but also a desire to eliminate the distance in the center in which consciousnesses move, distance that is not so much a type of preexisting framework, as what arises from those same presences to the degree in which they are separated one from another. Distance is not a property of an unknown space: it is the dimension of the human."[1] Following this line of thought, in a situation of full human dimensionality, distance itself would acquire a full human dimensionality. This is the experience that Swedenborg uses in his reduction of space to consciousness.

Therefore, Swedenborg gives so much importance to the theme of distance in its spiritual space because distance, as Brun states, is a specifically human dimension, which demonstrates how even physical space is unthinkable without the presence of these qualitative categories: distance humanizes and spiritualizes space.[2] Hence the subsumption of spatial distances to feelings and affections; or, if you like, the conversion, according to Swedenborg, of space into inner temporality, since in the spiritual regions (where spontaneity and liberty prevail) space—and consequently distance—is conditioned by the experiences of the soul. The more love and wisdom, the closer one is to the object; the less love and wisdom, the farther one will be from the object. This space that Swedenborg describes to us is the complete opposite of the Stoics' conception of space as indiscernible or of space as an a priori given of the senses. Space, for Swedenborg, is not distinguished from experience or reduced to experience. It is as if space had made itself purely qualitative, or as if we were before a pure spatial heterogeneity: all spatial relations are due to a transformation of consciousness. These concepts of heterogeneous space (space that is cultural, sacred, and ritual versus homogenous or profane) demonstrate the line of thought where Swedenborg's experience of inner space may be inserted.[3]

If we use Kierkegaard's definition of myth—"Mythology consists of maintaining the idea of eternity with the categories of time and space" (which is the best definition that we know)—we can perfectly express that when speaking of the categories of time and space Swedenborg is really speaking of eternity (the sphere of spirituality, the super-worldly, etc.). On the other hand, we must keep in mind the existing propensity to reduce time to space, possibly because the experience of time has an irreducible quality.[4] Clearly, what Swedenborg relates to us in his characteristic manner is the internal duration of consciousness, of heterogeneous time versus the homogeneous temporality of external time.

Time is what happens in us, and so it is irreducible; what we measure is movement in space. However, there is a propensity to express temporal instantiations under the form of spatial instantiations, due to the tendency in our spirit to equate space and time.[5] From this perspective, Swedenborg expresses what happens in him in spatial terms and concepts, the time of consciousness. Consequently, the movements of consciousness are expressed in terms of duration. These interactions between time and space should not seem strange to us, as a minimal analysis of concepts such as eon *(aion)* and *olam* shows us. In fact, eon is primarily indefinite time, eternity (in this sense it would oppose *kairos)*. Hence it comes to mean a qualitative and personalized state or space, a mediating hypostasis, or representative figures from the intelligible world. Something similar occurs with the Hebrew term *olam,* which shifts from meaning indefinite time and eternity to becoming more spatialized, meaning world, space, or situation. The same occurs with the Aramaic equivalent of *olam, alma,* and with the Arabic equivalent *alam;* both shift in meaning from time to mean qualitative space, states of spirit (remember the importance in Arabic philosophy of the notion of *'alam al-mizal,* the *mundus imaginalis,* as Henry Corbin translates it, the ontological and spiritual region mediating between the purely material and the purely intelligible). Likewise, in the expressions "present eon" and "in the eon to come" (with their Hebrew parallels *olam hazeh* and *olam ha-ba*) we find a much more profound sense than that of mere place: these expressions refer to global situations of humans, to spiritual states. And if the series *aion–olam–alma–alam* shows a temporality that spatializes, in the case of the Hebrew term *macon* we have a spatial notion that temporalizes. *Macon* (place, *topos*) comes to be considered an attribute of divinity—if not divinity itself— inasmuch as the "place" where the presence of the sacred is given is a living place, a full place of experience and temporality. In fact, the series *macon–topos* incorporates and assimilates the notion of chronos (time), and so by means of synecdoche the word *macon* is extrapolated, or its equivalents *topos–chronos*, as proper noun for God.⁶ That is, in all these cases we have an interpenetration of temporality and spatiality in manifestations of spiritual experiences. Broadly speaking, space is temporalized and time is spatialized. All this can be applied to Swedenborg and to his religious experiences. Phenomenologically speaking, Swedenborg's thought participates in philosophical, theological, and symbolic themes similar to those of other spiritual currents, possibly because the experience that sustains them is also similar. The internalizing of time and space and the reduction of such notions to experiences of the soul form a symbolic paradigm, like a language, of the phenomenology of the visionary consciousness.

Another element that we cannot forget and that constitutes an essential part of this consideration of time and space is that of personalization. All that we have stated regarding the terms *aion–olam–macon–chronos* occurred in philosophical-religious contexts in which personalization is the actual object of philosophical-religious reasoning. Significantly, personalization is a category that is also fundamental to Swedenborg's thought, since for him the universal movement of reality advances toward its ontological consummation, which is valued in the acquisition of personal instantiations. It is not inconsequential, then, that the specific realm of human spirituality (the actual representation of personalization) assumes personal aspects, when not reduced to actual personalization.

We emphasize the characteristic of personalization because it does influence the evolution of the category of eon. A specific state of being corresponds to a person that embodies or is that ontological mode; and for each specific person there is a specific time that is that very person (that is the sense of the various hypostases of the gnostic, Neoplatonic, and other similar systems). In Swedenborg, the presence of the category of personalization shows, among other things, the importance of the action of the subject in the configuration of reality. Thus, personalization, determination, and the human subject are correlative notions in the philosophy of the Prophet of the North: spiritual fullness passes through the three of them, and the three of them lead to this fullness.

We find ourselves here with one of Swedenborg's essential conceptions, one in which the "geography" of the spiritual world (*mundus imaginalis*, as Henry Corbin would say), the categorizing and foundation of the noetic sphere, is not resolved through fundamental concepts, but rather through states of the soul (again, the personalizing note). The affections of the soul—and the spiritual world is itself a soul—are those that generate their own space (internal space, of course), whose measures and distances are the variations of the soul itself and of its action (the *dilatatio mentis* of the medieval mystics), or in Swedenborg's terminology, *elongari et contrahi* (lengthened and shortened). Thus we have here an ontology of mediation, an ontology that is neither purely spiritual nor noetic, neither purely material nor perceptible, but rather one that makes the spiritual or noetic appear in order to become perceivable, one that spiritualizes the material and perceptible as it elevates them. In a word, it is about the ontology of the Creative Imagination.[7] We need to keep in mind, on the other hand, that Swedenborg locates spiritualized space precisely where ontological fullness causes consciousness to enjoy the spontaneity that is typical of that state. That space is not seen as determined by the external, but rather by that which conditions the external: we find ourselves in the sphere of the *intimum* (inmost). If we had to establish a general phenomenology of Swedenborg's work, we would say that it consists entirely of achieving and accepting the *intimum* of reality. "Since the highest thing in sequential arrangement is the central thing in simultaneous arrangement and the lowest is the outermost, 'higher' in the Word means more internal and 'lower' means more external" (*Divine Love and Wisdom* §206).

Love and Wisdom, Good and Truth form the categories—that is, the affections—fundamental to the spiritual world, and therefore the degree of their intensity marks the distance of the soul from the Lord. So for Swedenborg, spiritual locations are nothing other than symbols of the dynamics of consciousness, shown in correspondence with its ontology of representation.

I have stated that in the spiritual world, just as in this physical world, we can see space and therefore distances as well, but that they are appearances, dependent on spiritual likenesses of love and wisdom, or of what is good and true. This is why even though the Lord is with angels everywhere in heaven, he still appears high overhead, looking like a sun. Further, since it is the acceptance of love and wisdom that causes likeness to him, if angels have a closer resemblance because of their acceptance, their heavens appear to be closer to the Lord than those of the angels whose resemblance is more remote. (*Divine Love and Wisdom* §10)

We have, then, an internalization of time and space (or a reduction of space to time, inasmuch as time signifies duration of consciousness), that remain thus converted to states of the soul. This dynamic and plastic nature of consciousness, which generates its own space and its own time, is fundamental for comprehending a great part of the visionary narratives of all religions. It is quite clear, then, that for Swedenborg the geography of the spiritual world is symbolic and internal, that is, it is a matter of a geography of the visionary soul that lives the events that occur in its own consciousness. Therefore, there is a phenomenalization of this spiritual world in the consciousness that experiences that same world and its symbolic representations. All this varied morphology that Swedenborg and his visionary narratives present us is in reality the varied morphology of the soul and its representations. We see how, as with time and space, distances are subordinated to internalization. Since distances are themselves internal and spiritual, they will depend on each subject's capacity for love or wisdom. This internalization of locations is presented to us as another hermeneutical key for understanding not only Swedenborg, but all narratives of this type: space is utilized by converting itself into affections of the spirit.[8]

Since the east is the basis on which all the regions in the spiritual world are laid out, and since the east in the highest sense means the Lord and divine love, we can see that the Lord and love for him is the source of everything. We can also see that to the extent that people do not share in that love, they are far from him and live either in the west or in the south or in the north, with the distance depending on their openness to love. (*Divine Love and Wisdom* §122)

It makes sense that a particular openness to love and wisdom establishes a region in the spiritual world, given the fact that angels
change their location in response to any increase or decrease of love
in them. . . . The same holds true for us as far as our spirits are concerned. In spirit, each of us is in some particular region of the
spiritual world no matter where we may be in the physical world.
(*Divine Love and Wisdom* §126)

In short, this space comes to mean the dynamic and fluid character
of the spiritual world, where things are *non sint fixa et stata* (not static
and stable). "[T]he whole spiritual world is just like the whole physical
world, the sole difference being that things there are not static and stable the way they are in a physical world because there is nothing of nature there. Everything is spiritual" (*Divine Love and Wisdom* §321).[9] In
reality, what Swedenborg expresses in his works are the experiences of
the soul; the dynamics of the spirit itself; the extensions of qualitative
substance; the expansions, the flows, and the formalizations of the soul
in its being and in its working.

In summary, in a spiritual state it is internalization that conditions
spatiality, and location depends on the spiritual situation of the subject. It is the internal state of the soul that creates its own space or
world. Space is internalized; it has become "inner time." The categories that fall under the domain of spatial-temporal coordinates are reduced to affections and forms of the soul. Thus, space is love, time is
wisdom, color is goodness, light is the truth of the faith, and so on. In
Swedenborg a generalized internalizing of reality is presented, which is
a spiritual interpretation of reality, the form of this reality present and
acquired in the human soul. The quantitative differences fade away before the qualitative intensity of the forms in the consciousness. Heaven
in its entirety is an angel, the entire church is a human being; there is a
reduction of totalities (in a quantitative sense) to intensified consciousness. We can infer, then, the theory of the intensification of the forms
by the soul; that the principle of individualization lies in the form; that
the driving force that substantially motivates the assimilation of forms
is love; that the human form is the form of every bit of thought that
proceeds from celestial love.

With all this in mind, we can conclude that internalization is a fundamental parameter for the comprehension of Swedenborg. In effect, every category of Swedenborg's thought is internalized or undergoes a process of internalization. Therefore, concepts such as heaven, time, space, spiritual world, *homo maximus,* and church are seen as being reduced to inwardness, to experiences of the soul. Or, in other words, they lose their quantitative characteristics in order to take on other, purely qualitative ones. So there is no contradiction between the instantiations with collective meaning (such as the church, for example) and those that refer to the concrete individual: the church is a state of the soul, and so one person alone can be the church. As Swedenborg puts it:

> We can say the same of the church as we have of heaven, since the church is the Lord's heaven on earth. (*Heaven and Hell* §57)

> It is not the Word but the understanding of it that forms the church; and the quality of the church is determined by the way people in it understand the Word. (*True Christianity* §243)

> The church is within and not outside, and anyone is a church in whom the Lord is present in the qualities of love and faith. (*Heaven and Hell* §57)

This question serves as a sample of a general tendency of radically spiritual Christian religiosity: the primacy of a purely internal church, invisible, versus the external and visible church.[10] In similar fashion, an angel can be heaven and a person can be the Great Human. Since we are not dealing with quantifiable elements, the assumption of the qualitative substance allows the communication of language between the universal and the particular. All in all, it is internalization that will determine the ontological situation of the subject, and we need to realize that for Swedenborg an angel is nothing more than a person in which internalization completely predominates.

5

SOME CLARIFICATIONS REGARDING THE CONCEPT OF *Ecclesia* IN SWEDENBORG

The ascendancy that Swedenborg obtained in Romanticism in general, and the Romantic idea of the spiritual church in particular, is in our estimation at least partly due to his notion of *ecclesia* (church). The concept of *ecclesia* seems to us decisive for understanding Swedenborg's thought as a whole. For this reason we believe it is of interest to clarify this theme as much as possible.

As is known, for Swedenborg there were four churches (five, counting the current one) that serve for the establishment of historic periods. These churches are: the *Antiqissima ecclesia* (Most Ancient Church), the *Antiqua eccelsia* (Ancient Church), the *Ecclesia repraesentativa* (commonly called the Israelite or Jewish Church), the *Ecclesia christiana* (Christian Church), and the New Church or *Nova hierosolymitana*. Each of these churches can be defined by a certain way of interpreting, internalizing, and experiencing divine revelation. The *Antiqissima ecclesia* would be the Adamic or celestial church, the one most directly connected to the deep meaning of revelation: the one that speaks the language of the angels—that is, their direct, transparent language—without mediation. Therefore, of the four biblical styles, the one that corresponds to this primordial *ecclesia* is the one that is expressed as a symbolic history (the first seven chapters of Genesis), that is internal and in keeping with a direct experience of divinity. Later comes the *Antiqua ecclesia*, the spiritual or Noachian church, which already assumes a certain distancing from the pure, direct experience of the revealed message (the notion of *ecclesia* in Swedenborg is inseparable from his hermeneutics of profound meaning), although it continues communicating in a type of divine language (the spiritual, one level less profound than the celestial) through representations and correspondences. This *ecclesia* we see in Genesis 8–11. The third *ecclesia*, Israelite or *repraesentativa*, is a continuation of the one before, but much more external. The people of this church have taken one more step toward forgetting the meaning of correspondences and representations (of internalization, that is), to the point that it leads to idolatry. The *Ecclesia christiana* came to reestablish the profound meaning of the Word and its spiritual vividness, and with this put an end to the decadence that had developed since the *Antiqua ecclesia*. However, the *Ecclesia christiana* was gradually falling into a purely formal exteriority. This made necessary a new revelation, or the New Church, which in reality was nothing more than the unveiling of the profound sense of the Word for its complete internalization.

Thus, according to what can be deduced from this brief sketch, the idea of *ecclesia* in Swedenborg does not have any canonical or institutional meaning, but rather it is above all a state of the soul, either collective or individual. This state is brought about by interpreting the innermost sense of the Bible—the spiritual or celestial—or by *not* interpreting this sense. That is to say: *ecclesia* is determined by hermeneutics, since *ecclesia* (as well as the hermeneutics) is, above all, an inner experience and the opening of meaning. As a result, *ecclesia* is a spiritual and mystical reality, although with an obvious projection over the sphere of the visible world (in fact, the presence of *ecclesia* in this world is what makes it possible for humans to receive revelation, and with this the conjoining of humans with God). In line with this, all the theologemes related to the category of *ecclesia* in Swedenborg are equally internalized. Let us not forget that for our author, the dichotomies interior/exterior or literal sense/spiritual sense are universals. The final judgment is a judgment "in heaven," that is, spiritual and invisible, occurring in the sphere of consciousness, and the apocalypse is precisely that—the revelation of the internal sense of Scripture. We find ourselves, then, in the sphere of attained eschatology, where the events described in the book of Revelation (a book to which Swedenborg significantly dedicated a great number of exegetical pages) take place in the souls of the people who bring about in themselves the spiritual experience of manifestation (Last Judgment, New Earth, New Heaven, etc.). What occurs on the individual plane also happens on the collective plane, and this is the *ecclesia*. It is an internal and spiritual experience, invisible in itself (although able to be extrapolated) and having consequences in the external sphere. "There is no purely spiritual nor purely natural Church," according to Swedenborg. The *ecclesia* in the Swedenborgian sense, like all spiritual realities (heaven or angelic societies), presents two dimensions, one monadological and another associative. By this we mean that the *ecclesia* as qualitative reality, susceptible to intensive increases and decreases, can be predicated equally on an individual level or on the collective. An individual is *ecclesia* to the extent that he or she fulfills the essential characteristics of *ecclesia*, without any contradiction between the *ecclesia* as individual dimension (the church is a regenerated human) and the communitarian dimension, both of them inhabiting a purely qualitative state.

The concept of *ecclesia* in Swedenborg does not have a legal-ecclesiastical sense, but rather is open and dynamic: the *ecclesia* can grow or shrink in its spiritual constitution according to its reception of divine influx. This spiritual growth correlative to *ecclesia* depends on the degree of the appropriation of meaning on the part of the *eccelsia* in question, which is the same as saying that it depends on the level of internalization. *Ecclesia* as a spiritual reality is in solidarity with spiritual hermeneutics. An individual or community can be more of a church in that they reach a more profound sense of the Word, in that they internalize more. Keep in mind that Swedenborg's exegesis assumes a radical subjectivization of biblical narratives: these are above all narratives of the soul, taking place in all living souls. Naturally, all the fundamental categories of Swedenborg's thought become visible in his ecclesiology; thus, organicism, vitalism, teleologism, interior dynamism, and so on are ideas that characterize and define the ecclesial dynamic: every one pours into the all-encompassing concept of internal experience as a fundamental attribute of the idea of *ecclesia*. All that we have just stated is fulfilled by antonomasia with the New Church, or the ultimate and definitive church, revealed after the most recent divine judgment. According to Swedenborg, this divine judgment occurred in 1757, coinciding with his extreme existential crisis (and is not every crisis a judgment?). Evidently, Swedenborg does not understand this final judgment as applying to the material world, but rather from a perspective of fulfilled eschatology. He insists that eschatological events be interpreted spiritually, since they "happen" in the spiritual world (that is, they affect the inner disposition of the believer):

> The state of the world from now on will be exactly as it has been up to the present. This is because the immense change that has taken place in the spiritual world does not impose any change on the earthly world as to its outward form. . . . As for the state of the church, though, that is what will not be the same from now on. Oh, it will be the same in outward appearance, but it will be different as to what lies within. (*Last Judgment* §73)

In fact, the founding of the New Church does not mean the founding of another visible and external Christian confession, but rather the opening of the profound sense of Scripture so the believer can have a complete comprehension of its essential content. Thus, the New Church (or Church of the New Jerusalem, in reference to the book of Revelation) is a spiritual and internal reality. It is the revelation of the symbolism of the Word and its reception by the consciousness. As can be seen, the New Church is susceptible to being interpreted (in the Romantic fashion) in terms of the Church of Saint John, the invisible church, versus the exterior and visible Christian Church (predating Swedenborg's vision and interpretation of the Last Judgment), which would be equivalent to the Church of Saint Peter. Therefore, it seems legitimate to consider the notion of *ecclesia* in Swedenborg as an antecedent to the idea of church as *sacramentum salutis*.

We will now attempt to summarize and synthesize some of the principal features of Swedenborg's concept of *ecclesia,* as well as some of its consequences. Swedenborg's ecclesiology is filtered by its hermeneutics: the *ecclesia* will become even more spiritual as the reception of the Word is more spiritual or, in other words, they will be revealed as the deeper meanings are penetrated. With the New Church (and we must add, with the new revelation-interpretation, since both ideas are connected), the dynamics of externality end, and the internal focus begins to predominate. From here one can extrapolate these essential ecclesial categories to the sphere in which words such as esoteric, exoteric, and visible and invisible church acquire meaning. That is to say, these concepts are susceptible to being appropriated by Romantics or by those of a similar sensibility.

The way in which one understands the Word conditions the form of one's being, and from there we have the gradation of churches. Undoubtedly in Swedenborg there is a periodization of history by virtue of the types of churches or the ways of receiving and interpreting the Word. However, each *ecclesia* can also be understood as the disposition of each person in the presence of the reception and interpretation of the Word: how each one interprets and lives the text will determine to which *ecclesia* one belongs, or even if one will form one's own *ecclesia*, since the term *ecclesia* designates a spiritual and qualitative reality where unity and totality do not contradict each other. *Ecclesia* presents a monadological dimension (each person is a reality to the degree in which the person fulfills the content of that reality) and also a holistic dimension. We could, therefore, perfectly apply the description of kathenotheism (frequently used by Henry Corbin in reference to a means of conceiving Divinity) to this quality of *ecclesia* in the Swedenborgian sense: the *ecclesia* is one in each one of us. In the periodization of the different churches there is more than one order of succession, but also simultaneity, since each of us will belong to the *ecclesia* that our own soul experiences or lives. Naturally, this simultaneity will happen in a fundamental way between the Christian Church (the diverse confessions in the visible institutions) and the Christian New Church. That is, one belongs to one or another *ecclesia* according to one's experience and interpretation of the Word, whether it be external or internal, literal or spiritual.

Another very important consequence of what we have seen is Swedenborg's intuition of fulfilled eschatology regarding the idea of *ecclesia*. Since each *ecclesia* signifies not just a historical period, but also—and fundamentally—a way of interpreting the Word and a state of the soul, the relationship between the churches and other elements can be amplified. For example, for each *ecclesia* there are corresponding events in the Word, because each church will have an apocalypse and a last judgment, each church interpreting the eschatological events according to its way of adopting Scripture. A spiritual church will interpret the eschatological terms in a spiritual way, as happening "in the present" of whomever accepts such an event.

In Swedenborg we perceive many other intuitive ideas on this topic. One of them lies in the "theology of the remnant," tied to the idea of tradition as *ecclesia*. Because *ecclesia* is God's way of communicating with humans, he always preserves the *ecclesia* no matter how corrupt it becomes, through a "remnant" that maintains the original tradition. The "remnant" serves as a bridge between the church of the past and the church of the future: Noah, Abraham, Moses, and so on. The ideas of *ecclesia* and "remnant" are linked with the ideas of pristine revelation and tradition.

We close with a quote from Swedenborg: "It is not the Word that makes the church, but the way the Word is understood and that the quality of the church depends on the quality of the understanding of the Word for the people who are in the church" (*Sacred Scripture* §76).

In conclusion, I would like to delineate some possible areas of investigation for this topic. Swedenborg's conception of *ecclesia* is, above all, a manifestation of the idea of *homo maximus*, which in our judgment is about the image—let us not forget that in Swedenborg everything tends to become a concrete form, an image—of the theological category of mystical body of Christ. Here, in the idea of the mystical body of Christ, is where all of Swedenborg's speculation regarding the Church comes together. Therefore, we again find our author as a precursor to this theological notion in Romanticism.

6

THE TWO FORMS OF RELIGIOSITY IN THE *Journal of Dreams*

Swedenborg's *Journal of Dreams* is a fundamental document for understanding the work and life of Emanuel Swedenborg, since it reflects the transition from his scientific stage to the theological stage.[1] In the *Journal of Dreams* Swedenborg relates his spiritual experiences from 1743 and 1744, those which led him to dedicate his life completely to his theological work. The *Journal of Dreams* is the only book (with the exception of a few booklets of his youth) that Swedenborg wrote in Swedish. It is written in a carefree style, full of Latinisms and gallicisms, possibly because the author never thought about publishing it. This fact, and the sincerity and spontaneity with which Swedenborg narrates his experiences, makes the *Journal of Dreams* a priceless text. The *Journal of Dreams* remained unpublished until 1859, more than eighty years after the death of the author. After various vicissitudes, the manuscript had ended up in the Royal Library of Stockholm, where it was discovered and edited by librarian G. E. Klemming.[2] Its title can be deceiving: it begins as a diary of a journey, but later relates oneiric experiences together with visions in a state of wakefulness. The *Journal of Dreams* is one of the highest specimens of Christian spirituality, and it reveals the depth of the author's soul.

Our theory about the *Journal of Dreams* is that there are two spiritual experiences present in the book. One is of shamanic character, by means of which Swedenborg has bilocations, out-of-body experiences, visions, etc. These experiences tend to happen in conjunction with respiratory exercises of the type found in yoga. It seems that Swedenborg had had these types of experiences since he was young. Another important element of the numinous dimension consists in the internalization of the anatomy and his conversion to phenomenology of the astral body:

> It seemed as if I took a key and went in; the doorkeeper examined the keys I had; I showed them all, in the case I should have two, but it seemed that Hesselius had another. I was arrested and put under guard. Many went to see me. I thought I had done nothing wrong, but I realized that I might be put in an unfavorable light if it turned out that I had taken the key. I awoke. There may be various interpretations, such as that I have taken the key to anatomy, while the other one that Hesselius had was the key to medicine; or that the key to the lungs is the pulmonary artery, and thus to all the motions of the body; or, spiritually. (Night of March 25–26, 1744)[3]

In the *Journal of Dreams* we find many references to historical persons related to the life and times of Swedenborg. Johan Hesselius (1687–1752) was a physician, assessor in the Medical College, and a member of the Academy of Sciences. Thus, he was a scientific authority of his time. We appreciate here how the process of internalization of the human body is initiated in order to be transformed in the spiritual reality of the *homo maximus* (as Lars Bergquist insightfully suggests, we are in the presence of a spiritualization of *Regnum Animale*, Swedenborg's final scientific work). It is also interesting to note how Swedenborg attempts to rationalize his own dreams by means of his explanations.

The phenomenology of the astral body in Swedenborg is important not only for delimiting the type of ecstatic vision he undergoes (and which he records in the *Journal of Dreams*), but also is essential for understanding the evolution of Swedenborg's thought. The idea of *homo maximus,* characteristic of his theological phase, is implicit in the *Journal of Dreams* to the degree in which this document reveals the internalization of the anatomical and physiological categories that appear in *Regnum Animale* (at the time this dream was recorded Swedenborg had just published the first two volumes of the three-volume work) and also his spiritual conversion. Ultimately one would need to associate this whole series of ideas with the notion of mystical body of Christ:

> Was all night in a dream: I can recollect only a little, it was as if I was being instructed the whole night on various subjects, of which I cannot recall anything. I was asleep for nearly eleven hours. As far as I remember, something was mentioned of (1) substantial or essential things, which one should seriously search for; and of (2) thymus gland and *glandula renalis,* from which I conclude: just as the thymus sorts out the impure serum of the blood and *glandula renalis* remit into the blood that which has been purified, something similar might go on within us spiritually. (Night of April 11–12, 1744)[4]

We have alluded to the importance of respiration in Swedenborg's ecstatic experience, which is similar to that of the shaman or to yoga. In addition, this act is related, as we have stated earlier, to Swedenborg's training as an anatomist and to the process of internalization that we see already initiated here. In *Regnum Animale,* he posits among other things respiration as a type of communication between the spiritual substance and the body (Swedenborg was, at this time, very preoccupied with the Cartesian problem of the relationship between body and soul).

> I noticed it to be a fact—as, indeed, I had been inspired to think during the day and as was also wonderfully represented to me by a kind of luminous writing—that the will has the greatest influence on the understanding. When we inhale, the thoughts fly into the body, and when we exhale, the thoughts are in a peculiar way expelled and rectified; so the very thoughts possess their alternations of activity like the respiration of the lungs. For the inspiration belongs to the will and the expiration to nature, so that the thoughts have their alternations in every turn of respiration because, when wicked thoughts entered, I had only to draw the breath, whereupon they ceased. Hence, from this may also be seen the reason that, when in deep thought, the lungs are kept in a state of equilibrium and at rest, more according to nature, and that the inhalations are then faster than the expirations, when at other times the reverse is the case; and, furthermore, that a person in

ecstasy holds the breath, the thoughts then being as it were absent. Likewise in sleep, when both the inhalation and the expiration are governed by nature, when that is represented which inflows from above. The same may be deduced from the brain, that by the inhalation all the internal organs together with the brain itself are expanded, and that the thoughts thence have their origin and flux. (Night of April 12–13, 1744)[5]

It seems that Swedenborg speaks of a trance of the yogic or shamanic variety, which includes the symbolization of the external body as an image of the internal. This has its parallels with the anthropologies of the astral body. Facing phenomena such as these, Régis Boyer has attempted to connect Swedenborg with the ecstatic experiences of the traditional Scandinavian religions in his article "Swedenborg et l'ame scandinave" ("Swedenborg and the Scandinavian Soul").[6] It seems very problematic to prove this hypothesis, but undoubtedly this typology of raptures, ecstasies, and out-of-body experiences shows us in full the phenomenology of religions; we have sought to summarize this under the name of shamanism. It seems legitimate to speak of a certain spiritual experience in the *Journal of Dreams* that responds to the characteristics of ecstatic consciousness. That is, undoubtedly, a form of religiosity. However, in the *Journal of Dreams* there is also another form of spirituality and religious sensibility.

Finally, to finish this brief exposition of some of these experiences that follow a shamanic phenomenology, we will show a case of out-of-body experience that Swedenborg experienced in his crisis of 1744. We find here a theme typical of Swedenborg: the dilemma posited between two opposites, here characterized as the inward person *(inwertes menniskian)* and the outward *(atweretes)*:

Something strange happened to me: I got strong shivers, like those I had when Christ granted me his divine grace, one after another, ten or fifteen in a row. I expected to be thrown on my face like the last time, but this did not happen. At the last shiver, I was lifted up; and, with my hands, I felt a back. I touched the back all over and the chest underneath. Soon, it lay down, and I saw on the front a face, but quite obscurely.... This occurred in a vision, when I was neither asleep nor awake, because all my thoughts were composed. It was the inward human, separated from the outward, who experienced this. When I was wide awake, such shivers came over me several times. . . . God's grace is shown both to the inward and outward human in me; to God alone be praise and honor! From the following and other things, I notice that this means that I would perceive *veritates de sensationibus internis* [truths of internal sensations]. (Night of July 1–2, 1744)[7]

The other sphere alluded to in the *Journal of Dreams* is directly related to Christian religiosity. It is an experience that is explained from assumptions and propositions characteristic of a specifically Christian restlessness. We do not hesitate to label this sphere that appears in *Journal of Dreams* as mystical. We believe, although these two dimensions (the one we have called "shamanic" and the Christian one) are expressed in an inseparable manner in Swedenborg, they are, nevertheless, perfectly distinguishable. It is necessary to differentiate between them in order to achieve an accurate knowledge of Swedenborg's innermost longings. Swedenborg's experiences that resemble characteristics of yoga or shamanism could be paranormal; the experiences that fulfill purely Christian motivations are mystical. The name "natural mysticism" could be used for the first type of experience of which we speak, but it seems to us inadequate. At any rate, it is beyond the scope of this study to analyze comparative mysticism in detail. There are, then, two forms of spirituality, though we reiterate that they are habitually presented in a unified, or at least closely related, manner.

The specifically Christian part of Swedenborg's religiosity in the *Journal of Dreams* (and later in all his work) may be best defined by the attention given to Saint Paul's letter to the Romans. We do not believe that it is necessary to stress the key importance that this Pauline document has for the history of Christian spirituality. Swedenborg is fully inscribed into the tradition influenced by the book of Romans, and thus we see a reference to Romans in Swedenborg, specifically dealing with the issue created by Romans 5:5:

Easter day was on 5 April; and then I went to God's table. The temptation was persistent, mostly in the afternoon up to six o'clock. There was nothing definite, but an anxiety as if one were damned and in hell; and yet all the time remained in the hope which the Holy Ghost inspired; and very strongly so, according to Paul's Epistle to the Romans, 5:5. The evil one had power given him to produce inquietude in my innermost by various thoughts. On Easter day, after communion, I was inwardly content, but still outwardly distressed. The temptation came in the afternoon, in an entirely different manner, but strongly; for I was assured that my sins were forgiven, but yet I could not govern my wayward thoughts to restrain some expressions opposed to my better knowledge. It was from the evil one, by permission. Prayer gave some relief, and also the Word of God; faith was there entirely, but confidence and love seemed to be absent. (Night of April 5–6, 1744).[8]

We are standing before a crucial experience in Swedenborg's spiritual crisis: in an emblematic Resurrection Sunday, having spent a sleepless night on Holy Friday and Saturday and after communing in a pietistic church of The Hague (let us remember that Swedenborg was just visiting), our author emerges to the light of divine grace: this whole text is a manifestation of the step from anguish *(ängslann)* to grace *(nåd)*. The Eucharist (*Gudz bord,* literally the Divine Table) held great importance for the Moravian Brothers of Zinzendorf, a pietistic current that in those times exerted a strong influence over our Swedish author.

Here, in this sphere of profound and dramatic spirituality, we see the action of the Holy Spirit in helping us escape from the anguish produced by guilt and sin. New references to Romans appear on other occasions in Swedenborg's works. This is expected, given that the issue of free will occupies a transcendental place in our author's theological thought. The recurrence to Romans takes place to demonstrate, first of all, the necessity of the action of the Holy Spirit, and secondly, to emphasize the importance of works versus faith alone, thus, to affirm free will. Specifically, with no intention of being exhaustive, we see Romans 3:28 cited in *Revelation Unveiled* §417 and in a letter to Oetinger; likewise in *Divine Providence* §115. Another reference to Saint Paul (Col. 2:9) appears in a letter to Doctor Beyer[9] in relation to the humanity of Christ. All this is a clear demonstration of a Pauline inspiration, and thus an expressly Christian inspiration, for our author. This recurrence to Saint Paul generated by Swedenborg's defense of free will and by his postulation of the value of works is present in the *Journal of Dreams*, inundating it with his religious piety and demonstrating again that in this revelation of inwardness we find the principal themes that will be examined later. By means of example, we cite these words: "Therefore a faith without works is not the right kind of faith: one must really sacrifice oneself" (Night of April 21–22, 1744).[10]

Naturally, however, there are many theological motifs in the *Journal of Dreams* that show us a Christian experience on the part of the wise Swede. Certainly we cannot aim to examine all of them; we will refer to a few of them that are most fundamental. The first one that draws our attention is the Christ-centered piety that accompanies all of Swedenborg's inner experiences and that corroborates our thesis about the existence of a specifically Christian mysticism in his dream diary:

> I was all day in equivocal thoughts, which tried to destroy the spiritual by contemptuous abuse to the extent that I felt that the temptation was very strong. By the grace of the Spirit, I managed to focus my thoughts on a tree, then to the cross of Christ, and on to the Crucifixion; and as often as I did so, all other thoughts fell flat to the ground, as of by themselves. I pushed this thought so far, that it seemed to me I was pressing down the tempter by means of the cross and driving him away; and then, after a while, I was free. Afterwards, I had to fix my thoughts upon it so intently that, whenever I let it slip out of my thoughts and internal vision, I fell into temptation-thoughts. Praise be unto God, who has given me this weapon! May God of grace keep me in this, that I may always have my crucified Savior before my eyes. For I dared not look upon my Jesus, whom I have seen, because I am an unworthy sinner; but then I ought to fall upon my face. And it is Jesus who lifts me up to look upon him, and therefore, I must look upon Jesus crucified. (Night of April 13–14, 1744)[11]

Certainly these sensitive images could have resulted from the influence of the pietism of Zinzendorf, a congregation that strongly emphasized the sensual aspects of Christian devotion as a reaction to the Lutheran orthodoxy. However, as Bergquist himself recognizes, in Swedenborg's case it is a matter of figures and motifs characteristic of all Christian mystics. It is evident that the personality of Jesus Christ becomes the center of all genuine Christian reflection and spirituality, but even more in the case of the Scandinavian we see a piety that is moved by features that are sensual, bloody, and of his inner vision (*inwertes syn*) of Christ and not by any conceptual or abstract consideration. That is, Swedenborg would be placed within modern and corporealist mysticism, and that would affiliate him with the great mysticism of the Spanish Golden Age (of course, all this spirituality also comes about because Swedenborg wanted to react against the coldness of official Protestantism). We cite, by way of example, another paragraph of a Christ-centered character:

> I had a preternaturally good and long sleep for twelve hours. On awakening, I had before me Jesus crucified and his cross. The spiritual came upon me with all its heavenly, almost ecstatic life, and I was ascending so high and permitted to go higher and higher, that had I proceeded, I would have been dissolved by this veritable joy of life. It then appeared to me in the spirit that I had gone too far; that in my thoughts I had embraced Christ on the cross, when I kissed his feet and that I then removed myself thence, falling upon my knees and praying before him crucified. It seemed that the sins of my weakness are forgiven as often as I do this. It occurred to me that I might have the same idol before the eyes of my body too, but I found that this would be far from right and, indeed, a great sin. (Night of April 15–16, 1744)[12]

We need not argue further that the suffering humanity of Christ represents a fundamental element of Swedenborg's spirituality, a spirituality that we cannot doubt is mystic, however it appears in the *Journal of Dreams*. We believe the sincerity of these experiences is proven by the intense drama with which the author describes them to us. The following is an example:

> Now, while I was in the spirit and in [such] thoughts, I sought by means of my thoughts to gain a knowledge of how to avoid all that is impure; but I noticed that, every time something from the love of self intruded and was turned about in the thought—as, for instance, when someone did not show the proper regard for me according to my own

imagination—I always thought, "If you only knew what grace I am enjoying, you would act otherwise," which at once was something impure, having its source in the love of self. After a while, I perceived this and prayed God to forgive it; and then I desired that others might enjoy the same grace, and perhaps they possess it or will obtain it. Thus, I observed clearly that there was still with me that dreadful apple which has not yet been converted, which is the root of Adam and original sin; yes, and in addition to that, the roots of my sin are infinite in number. (Night of April 7–8, 1744)[13]

We find ourselves before a profound experience of the self, the depth of self-love *(grund af egen kerlek)*, as radical opposition to divine grace *(nåd)*. If the *Journal of Dreams* is a successive demonstration of oppositions that reveal Swedenborg's innermost conflict, here we find ourselves with the most unfathomable contraries: the self, the eternal root of sin *(oendelig annan rot jag har til synden)*, and the grace of God that comes to substitute for the root of human poverty. Undoubtedly, in this self-love taken as original sin, we see that category that will appear in later theological work: the *propium,* the fundamental obstacle that humans confront in their rescue by God, this depth of egotistical self-affirmation that all humans possess. This theme, found in the *Journal of Dreams,* will be more fully developed by Swedenborg later. The *Journal of Dreams* is a text that, because of its intermediate position, becomes a hermeneutical key to comprehending not only the first phase of Swedenborg's thought, but the second phase as well. With respect to Swedenborg's visions of the humanity of Christ, in other places we have spoken of the spirituality of Saint Teresa and of the sensibility of Pascal;[14] now this latest experience appears to us as an antecedent to some of Kierkegaard's meditations. This internal conflict that Swedenborg suffers during his existential crisis will be suffered by Kierkegaard in *Fear and Trembling (Frygt och Baeven,* 12–13). All this we supply as evidence of the specific Christian character of the mysticism of the *Journal of Dreams.*

There is a constant that dominates the sincere and precious document that is the *Journal of Dreams* (though, as we observed, there are not only dreams but also visions and ecstasies). We refer to the troubled state Swedenborg suffers in his innermost self, which is manifested in a pair of opposites, irreconcilable in this moment of profound personal crisis during the years 1743–44 but that he will try to reconcile in later works. It is beyond the scope of our project to cover all the implicit and explicit problems in this book we are examining now, because that would not be the object of our analysis. However, if we had to summarize in some form all these troubling oppositions to which we allude, we would do so by means of this citation: "Afterwards I went out and saw many black images; one was thrown to me. I saw that it had no use of its foot. This meant, I think, that natural reason could not accommodate to spiritual reason" (Night of March 25–26, 1744).[15]

In these words we can glimpse one of Swedenborg's typical dilemmas: natural reason versus spiritual reason (*esprit de géometrie* versus *esprit de finesse?*), a dilemma that will give rise to the later attempt at reconciliation but here acquires different variations: internal/external, *prima vita/altera vita, impurum/purum,* the force of the Spirit or grace *(andans kraft, nåd)* and our unworthiness or sin *(owärdighet, synd),* etc. These expressions that speak to us of a strong internal struggle among opposites, among equivocal or double thoughts *(dubla tanckar),* are constants throughout the *Journal of Dreams.* As Swedenborg states, "I was continually in dissention with double thoughts, opposed to one another" (Night of April 12–13, 1744).[16] All these dualities reveal the state of great spiritual turbulence in which Swedenborg found himself while writing this dream diary, a state that will provoke the abandonment of his scientific activity and the start of his theological work.

We have attempted to show the way in which two distinct—but not mutually exclusive—forms of spirituality coexist in the *Journal of Dreams.* One we call yogic or shamanic because of its phenomenological similarity to what we know of these types of experiences. It is based fundamentally on visions, out-of-body experiences, descriptions of the astral body, and the great importance of respiratory exercises.[17] The other class of spiritual experiences is marked by Christian patterns, and we have labeled those as mystical. We have cited some examples here that we believe support our opinion. Thus, the importance of Saint Paul and of the Pauline problem, the perceptible visions of a human and suffering Jesus Christ, the importance of the Eucharist, and the presence of a complete terminology that fully reveals a guiding nucleus of specifically Christian ideas: grace *(nåd),* infinite grace of God *(Gudz oendeliga nåd),* Holy Spirit *(helge ande),* and also expressions characteristic of mystical traditions *(centrum; per incomprehensibilem circulum a centro)*, and so on. All this indicates that the restlessness that moves Swedenborg is due to motives of the Christian variety, with a few clarifications needed. The *Journal of Dreams* is the product of a profound and painful existential crisis. The series of visions and ecstasies that are described here do not extend to Swedenborg's later work. The mystical experiences that he recorded for us in writing (although with no desire to have them published) begin and end in the *Journal of Dreams*. Many of the problems treated in the dream diary have their continuity (and their solution, in Swedenborg's eyes) in his theological work (the relationships of science/faith, body/soul, free will, etc.), but the mystical images and experiences are not repeated: they belong exclusively to the period of 1743–44. Certainly, in this period Swedenborg frequented in Stockholm, The Hague, and London the Herrnhutian centers of Baron von Zinzendorf, which represented then a form of Protestant religiosity that advocated affective and perceptible devotion over pure fideism. However, this influence alone does not explain the Christ-centeredness and the predominance of the will over the understanding that we find in Swedenborg. The force and the passion with which he describes his experiences transcend any possible circumstantial influence and are due ultimately to his inner spiritual experimentation. In addition, we need to say that in 1744 Swedenborg already begins to show his differences with respect to the Moravian Brothers.

Echoes of Baroque mysticism or of a *devotio moderna?* Anti-deist reaction? Undoubtedly, as with his original pietistic affiliation, they are factors that we must keep in mind when we want to explain Swedenborg's mystical phenomena, such as what appears in the *Journal of Dreams,* in order to clarify not only the visions based on his ecstatic capacity but also the speculative mysticism (which leads us to compare him at times with Saint Teresa).

Another reason that leads us to trust Swedenborg's experiences is the absolute lack of literary stylization in his dream diary, which he never thought about publishing and which he wrote in Swedish (all the work he published was written in Latin). A curious detail in this sense is that Swedenborg often uses Latin or even French for technical terms; it would be very crucial to study the Swedish words he uses, since they would undoubtedly reveal the deepest movements of his spirit. The narrative of his visions, dreams, and ecstasy is expressed in a chaotic and unsystematic way (and there are few authors as systematic as Swedenborg), following only the impulses and passionate movements of his soul.[18]

We have attempted to lay out the two forms of religiosity, or spirituality, or sensibility in the presence of the transcendental, that we find in the *Journal of Dreams*. We have hardly scratched the surface regarding these two phenomena, which occur in a critical moment of Swedenborg's life. The *Journal of Dreams*, which convincingly embodies that crisis, is a document that is very rich in content and possibility, vital as well as intellectual. With our approach we have attempted to signal some lines of investigation that no doubt would produce abundant results not only for the knowledge of Swedenborg's life, but also for the study of comparative mysticism in general.

7

REPRESENTATION AND CONCEPT
IN SWEDENBORG

The relationship between thought and literature, from a philosophical perspective, can be reduced to the relationship between representation and concept. Here we refer to the question of the very origins of philosophy. The dichotomy of representation and concept is a way of expressing the duality of myth and Logos.

Undoubtedly we have all read or heard at some time a reference to the origins of philosophy as "the transition from myth to Logos." This is, certainly, a very superficial view that is overcome by any amount of analysis. What do "myth" and "Logos" mean, exactly? Logos is a concept, and it always leads us to thoughts of the unintelligible. Logos means the essential determination of each thing, its reason and intelligibility. The discourse of Logos will be, then, a discourse where concept and unifier predominate.

Myth has the sense of history, narrative, story, poem. The verb *myzéomai* means, among many other things, to tell a story. Originally, then, neither the term myth nor the verb form from which it comes had the meaning of legend or chimera that we habitually attribute to myth. A myth is characterized fundamentally as a narrative, that is, a discourse conveyed by means of images and representations. Within this same order of things, we can establish a difference similar to that between *halaka,* or normative legal interpretation in Judaic exegesis, and the *haggadah* or narrative interpretation (the verb *nagad* also has the meaning, among others, of telling a story). Myth and Logos are not opposed to each other, but rather are two types of discourse or exposition of ideas. Mythical discourse is characterized by being narrative and representative (since it can be imagined); the discourse of Logos is characterized by being conceptual and unifying (its ideal is to unfold mathematically).

Clearly, in light of what we have stated, the origins of philosophy cannot be established in an alleged distinction between myth and Logos. On the contrary, we continually see in Greek philosophy—and later throughout the entire history of philosophy—how in the work of one thinker narrative discourses alternate with conceptual and purely intelligible elements. This is especially true of Plato, for whom myth fulfills the function of accessing places that concepts cannot reach. That is precisely the purpose of myths for Plato: to discursively express what for Logos is ineffable. There is no contradiction between myth and Logos, as Plato demonstrates (and who would doubt his rationality?); myth simply goes beyond Logos, reaching more profound depths of being and of consciousness than concept. In fact, myth is already Logos to the degree that myth itself introduces determination and organizes reality, unifying it and lending it coherence.

Plato is not, of course, the only example of this. Throughout the entire history of thought we see how philosophers rooted in conceptual thought have appealed to narrative and representation in order to be able to express in a more faithful manner the object of their reflection; or because the type of knowable experience that they want to transmit adapts better to narrative discourse than to logic. Thus Avicenna or Sohravardi, on the side of rigorously conceptual expositions, have written texts in which the transcendental order is lived as a decisive adventure: this is expressed in the dichotomy *falsafa/hikmat*. The poem of Parmenides (also a visionary tale) combines representative figures and ontological statements without a break in continuity. Philo of Alexandria explicitly introduces narrative as an object of philosophical analysis. Likewise, *Don Quijote and Sancho* in Unamuno or *Abraham and Don Juan* in Kierkegaard also tell us of the vicissitudes of Logos. They are myths, in the strictest sense of the word, that do not impede the determination of Logos but rather model and direct it into channels of meaning.

It is not just philosophical concepts or categories that are susceptible to being expressed in representative discourses. Any event or experience that has an especially relevant or profound meaning, one that affects the essence of the human being in a fundamental manner, tends to order itself into a narrative form. We could say that it needs to convert itself into narrative in order to acquire a constitutive form. A clear example of this is mysticism. In fact, mysticism as an experience of the ineffable requires a symbol that embodies the unattainable aspect of that experience; a symbol or metaphor that is converted into the privileged language of narrative, that in fact constitutes the very fabric of the visionary narratives of initiation.

From all this we deduce a certain preeminence of representative language over the conceptual, of the symbol over Logos. Thus René Guénon, in contrast with Hegel, believed that a philosophy cast in a symbolic mold (for him the Vedas and Indian thought in general) penetrates farther into the essence of reality than a philosophy that is developed within the limits of concept.

Myth is plural and varied in its dimensions. It stands in opposition to history in the sense that as alternatives to history's possibilities it presents paradigms or models that unify the dispersion of *fieri* (what Eugeni d'Ors called *eones*). The forms of narrative offer constants and archetypes for the perceptible. For example, the Epic of Gilgamesh (possibly humanity's oldest book) contains models that later will be repeated in historical manifestations. The narrative myth repeats a fundamental event and makes that event present through the act of repetition. In fact, both ontological necessity and mystical ineffability need narrative in order to organize and determine themselves in accessible, repeatable, and communicable expressions.

We will now attempt to show how what we have said with respect to the relationship between narrative and conceptual discourse is applicable to the case of Emanuel Swedenborg. This has two aspects: the first is to Swedenborg's work itself; the second is to the resonance of the visionary Swede in posterity. Regarding the former, we need to start by looking at the circumstances in which his theological and visionary works were created. After his existential crisis of 1743–44, Swedenborg abandoned his scientific work (which ranged from mathematics to anatomy) and dedicated himself to transcribing and systematizing his spiritual experiences, experiences that may very well be called mystical. Before this point he had produced an ample collection of scientific works, as described in the introduction. In this phase—dominated by scientific thought of the age, Aristotle, Descartes, and Wolff, among others—Swedenborg reveals little by little his uneasiness regarding spiritual issues (the relationship between body and soul, God and world, faith and works, etc.) that he could not resolve either by science, by Enlightenment rationalism, or by Lutheran theology. This situation leads him to a profound crisis, described in the book *Journal of Dreams*. From that point on, as we have stated, his theological work begins (consisting of expounding his visions in an orderly way), and it will occupy him the rest of his life: *Secrets of Heaven, Last Judgment, Revelation Unveiled, Marriage Love, True Christianity*, and many other works, some of them published posthumously.

However, we will not now begin a concrete analysis of any specific texts of Swedenborg's visionary experiences, nor of his theological system, which would be beyond our scope. We will, on the other hand, focus on the mode of expression and communication of that content. Significantly, the appearance of figurative elements in Swedenborg's work begins in the intermediate phase, that is, when he has the transcendental mystical experience that gives rise to his theological phase. One must speak unequivocally of an intermediate phase in the work of the wise Swede, a phase that serves as mediation between the scientific and theological phases; a phase that prolongs the categories and the earlier problems, but at the same time transfigures them: here is where he sows the seeds of his representative language in close relationship with his inner experiences. This intermediate phase would be reflected in his *Journal of Dreams* (as discussed in the previous chapter), and above all in *Spiritual Experiences* (which he began writing in 1745 and continued until 1765) since here Swedenborg records the narratives that later will appear in successive books. *Worship and Love of God* (begun before *Journal of Dreams* but published in London in 1745) occupies a significant position. In fact, *Worship and Love of God* signifies the culmination of his scientific phase and at the same time the recognition of its limits. This is shown in the very structure and language of the book: on the one hand *Worship and Love of God* pulls together physical and biological theories expounded in *Principia Rerum Naturalium, De Infinito,* and *Oeconomia Regni Animalis;* but on the other hand it incorporates a poetic and rhetorical language, full of images and allegories. The very fact that the work was never completed demonstrates the irresolvable problems, or at least troublesome problems, that it posits: it is not possible to answer the author's metaphysical and theological problems with a conceptual discourse; the new phase requires a transformation of language to the degree in which consciousness itself is transformed. Swedenborg is proclaiming the necessity of tapping into another type of discourse. It is the discourse of concept versus the discourse of image.

As we have stated many times, there is something essential and particular in Swedenborg related to the fact that the process of representation is carried out to the degree in which an exegetical process is developed: explanations, experiences, and representations form a single movement, since after all biblical interpretation consists of explaining representations. This is manifested in *Worship and Love of God* (in reality a Hexameron) and in *Spiritual Experiences,* both ultimately works of biblical hermeneutics.

Swedenborg's intermediate phase is characterized by an exhaustion of scientific and rationalist discourse, since this phase is a preparation for the assumed developments in the theological phase and for beginning his mystical experiences. The appearance of narrative discourse coincides with the appearance of visionary experiences. By means of this motif, Swedenborg confers literariness, because in order to describe his inner life he needs to use symbols as a privileged vehicle to express spiritual realities. In addition, the literary methodology is necessary because when one brushes against the Absolute, one changes language; the commonplace and routine no longer work. In this sense the words of H. Jürgen Baden seem to us very opportune:

> A person is struck by the lightning of faith; from this moment on his life is split into two halves, and he will speak of an old life and a new life. Both forms of life are so irremediably separated that the continuity of destiny and of name is merely formal. The convert perceives that between the present and the past, between the now and the then,

a chasm has opened up, he no longer understands his prior life, he knows he can never go back. With the conversion a new dimension of his destiny has been revealed to him; and in this manner a total change in the assessment of people, of things, and of events is produced.[1]

Thus, the new existential horizon requires a new language in which to express it.

For Swedenborg it is necessary, after the intermediate phase, to represent conceptual thinking and make it a figurative and schematic narrative. The hermeneutical key for understanding this aspect of Swedenborg's work lies in the word representation (*repraesentatio*), since it so happens that not only are natural realities representations of spiritual or celestial realities, but also that the latter themselves are representations, or at least they have to be represented in order to be known. Therefore the representations of the spiritual world have ontological density versus the fantasies and imaginations (*phantasiae, imaginationes*) that are characterized by having a phantasmagorical reality.[2] The representations constitute the metaphysics of reality; we could say the ontology of the good, of the essence, and of the figures of positivity. Meanwhile, fantasies constitute the metaphysics of the deliquescent entities in which the inessential prevails; we could say the ontology of evil and of darkness, of the forms of negativity. It is not simply that Swedenborg's language becomes representative, but rather that its very ontology becomes an ontology of the figure and of the representation. One could affirm that Swedenborg's scientific stage (with all its problematic aspects) requires the perspective of figurative schematization to acquire fullness and resolution.

We now need to apply what we stated earlier: Swedenborg's work requires a figurative narrative as the end point and fulfillment of the corresponding concepts from his scientific stage: the order of concepts versus the order of images.

In Swedenborg the flow and movement of consciousness in its spiritual adventure is determined through images and configurations (angels, qualitative time and space, spiritual bodies, astral distances and geographies, etc.). In the same way (and consequently) those determinations also solidify in a narrative discourse, and thus Swedenborg's theological concepts are represented as figures, not because they may be allegories, but because they are experienced truly as individual and personal figures and manifestations. Swedenborg needs to embody his experiences in a representative discourse because these very experiences are representative, because concept does not completely engulf them, and fundamentally because narrative offers him a model that structures and gives cohesion to the movements of interiority. Thus Swedenborg's literary expression is very important for correctly understanding his religious work. The narrative structure in Swedenborg is of the same essence as his own thought.[3] As stated earlier, Swedenborg's ontology is essentially one of representation and image (*mundus imaginalis, 'alam al-mizal,* utilizing formulas beloved by Corbin).

After his work *Revelation Unveiled,* published in 1766, Swedenborg introduces a variation in the way he describes his visions. We are referring to *memorabilia* (memorable occurrences), vividly narrated stories that the author introduces after purely theological discourses or chapters. The *memorabilia* stand out for their literary style and for their expressive elaboration. *Memorabilia* that appear in *Marriage Love* (1768) have a special tone, since the stylistic intention is more notable (that is, its literary character). Finally, as additions to *True Christianity* (1771), some of the visionary narratives reappear (for example, the situation or representation in the spiritual world of Luther, Melanchthon, Calvin, the Dutch, Germans, Catholics, Africans, Muslims, Jews, etc.).

In these narratives Swedenborg's tendency to represent and convert all ideas or concepts into images is clearly manifested. It is as if Swedenborg were reminding us of the necessity of appealing to mythopoetic imagery to construct a coherent religious vision because concepts alone do not suffice. In summary, there is a correlation between spiritual experience, ontology, and language that explains the use of narrative in Swedenborg.

The other aspect of Swedenborg we mentioned earlier is the influence that the visionary Scandinavian has had on posterity. The influence that is of most interest to us now is that which is reflected among literary writers, poets, and artists. In fact, the fascination that poets and writers in general have felt for Swedenborg is something worthy of reflection. It might seem an exaggeration to claim that Romanticism cannot be understood without Swedenborg, but if we consider the list of authors that in one way or another find themselves influenced by Swedenborg, then that affirmation becomes completely plausible: Novalis, Heine, Blake, Coleridge, Balzac, Almqvist, Emerson, Jung-Stilling, Flaxman, Carlyle, Gérard de Nerval, etc. To all of these we have to add Baudelaire and literary symbolism (to the point that Octavio Paz makes Swedenborg the creator of modern poetry). Later the list broadens to include names such as Dostoevsky, Jorge Luis Borges, Unamuno, Ekelöf, Ekelund, Strindberg, Eugeni d'Ors, Arnold Schönberg, Malcolm de Chazal, César Milosz, etc. All that without looking at Swedenborg's influence on philosophers such as Oetinger, Schubert, Schelling, or Krause, and on theologians of the New Church of the Lord (a creed created by some disciples of Swedenborg after his death).

What interests us now is Swedenborg's impressive influence on the lettered and artists, since they were fundamentally responsible for spreading Swedenborg's visionary ideas. We could say that this interest is due to what the poet sees in Swedenborg: someone who conveys his experiences of the transcendental not through abstract and conceptual categories (philosophemes or theologemes), but rather through concrete images and forms. Swedenborg is a thinker in whom narrative prevails over concept, and determination over abstract identity. Naturally, poets are more inclined to express their theological and metaphysical ideas in a figurative way than to use a vehicle belonging to the categorical sphere. Poets favor representation even when they want to establish a system of ideas. This is what happened in Romanticism. For the great Swedish poet Carl Jonas Love Almqvist, Swedenborg gave Romanticism the intellectual program that it needed, thus correcting its lack of concretization. But this program was developed not only with philosophical or theological ideas, but also with images and figures. In Swedenborg, we find narrative discourse together with the discourse of Logos, which in our judgment explains his influence over so many writers, above all Romantics. At this point we will not address the issue of the correctness of the Romantic reception of Swedenborg (but see chapter 10). The fact is that Swedenborg's narrative drove the narrative of a large number of writers and artists, not only as a literary motif (what Karl-Erik Sjöden called "literary Swedenborgianism"),[4] but also and fundamentally as a determinant and articulating model of ideas and experiences that otherwise would have been diluted or remained in the world of pure concept or of pure indetermination.

Swedenborg, then, posits assumptions of a religious, metaphysical, existential, and mystical nature. Yet he does not do this only through systematization (Logos). He frames all those assumptions within a narrated, imagined, and represented construction (myth). The poet captures the former through the latter and in the latter. This presence of Swedenborg among poets does not belong only to the past; it continues to our day. For example, Miguel Florián is one who has felt the Swedenborgian influence. Florián is a philosopher and poet (having written several books of poetry), which makes for a double motive for including the Prophet of the North in his work. We will now highlight a poem titled "Swedenborg," which comes from the book *Anteo:*

> *To his lips the angels descended*
> *with their wings of silver. They gave him*
> *with eternal words,*
> *marvelous fires, harmonies*
> *of planets, of music, of bonfires.*
> *In the streets of London, the murmur*
> *of wind announced the frost*
> *of its bodies, the whitest angels*
> *brought him gifts of another life,*
> *such as the elderly—so secret—*
> *that collect the light of midday.*[5]

This poem has obvious echoes of a superb sonnet by Jorge Luis Borges that is also about Swedenborg:

> *Taller than the rest, he walked*
> *That man distant among men.*[6]

It seems that no Borges specialist has caught on to this recurrence of Swedenborg throughout Borges's body of work. We believe that Swedenborg's ideas and experiences appear on the Argentine's horizon of metaphysical and religious possibilities, as we discuss in the next chapter. But returning to Miguel Florián, we believe that the motive for his poem is more literary than anything else. We have the impression that the underlying themes of Florián's poem are not philosophical or theological, but rather that this beautiful poetic text was inspired by the very name of Swedenborg, his air of the legendary, the certain aura of mystery that always accompanied him. With the exception of the angels, no direct reference to the fundamental and characteristic arguments of Swedenborg's work appear in the poem. We would be, then, in the presence of an example of Sjöden's "literary Swedenborgianism" (this without signifying any lack of sincerity in the literary act itself).

We turn now to another writer that likewise has utilized Swedenborg as a theme for a poem. We speak of Carlos Liscano and of his book *Miscelleanea observata* (*Miscellaneous Observations*):

> *Emanuel Swedenborg was a man of system.*
> *In his house of Hornsgatan, in downtown Stockholm,*
> *Emanuel spoke with the angels.*
> *To explain an idea he met with Leibniz in heaven*
> *twenty years after the death of Leibniz.*
> *Swedenborg was right.*
>
> *(Stubborn birds of winter*
> *sing in the dead forest)*[7]

Is Liscano's use of Swedenborg a mere literary device? As in other cases, an explanation based only on literary formalism does not satisfy us. In the poems of Miguel Florián, Carlos Liscano, or even in those of Borges, though there is not an explicit declaration of Swedenborgianism, we hear echoes of metaphysical desire and unattainable pulsations toward the transcendent. In short, resonating in those texts is something that can be expressed only through the narrative of discourse, or, equally, through myth.

8

SWEDENBORG IN HISPANIC LITERATURE

Swedenborg and Miguel de Unamuno

Emanuel Swedenborg has not been an author who has had much luck in Spain. Unlike France, England, or Germany, there has been no penetration of the ideas of the Swedish thinker among Spaniards. Thus, we are surprised by the citations of Swedenborg in *Del sentimiento trágico de la vida* (*The Tragic Sense of Life*, 1913) by Miguel de Unamuno (1864–1936).[1] But this fact, being in itself unusual and worthy of mention, acquires a notable value if we keep in mind the aptness and justness of Unamuno's references to Swedenborg. Let us examine some of them.

Three are explicit citations. The first of them refers to an essential theme in Swedenborg: personalization as a fundamental determination of reality.

And neither ought we to be surprised by the affirmation that this consciousness of the Universe is composed and integrated by the consciousnesses of the beings that form the Universe, by the consciousnesses of all the beings that exist, and that nevertheless it remains a personal consciousness distinct from those that compose it. Only thus is it possible to understand how in God we live, move, and have our being. That great visionary, Emanuel Swedenborg, saw or caught a glimpse of this in his book on heaven and hell (*Heaven and Hell* §52), when he tells us: "An entire angelic society appears sometimes in the form of a single angel, which also it hath been granted me by the Lord to see. When the Lord himself appears in the midst of the angels, he doth not appear as encompassed by a multitude, but as a single being in angelic form. Hence it is that the Lord in the Word is called an angel, and likewise that an entire society is so called. Michael, Gabriel, and Raphael are nothing but angelical societies, which are so named from their functions."[2]

Later Unamuno says, in the same mode of interpretation:

> May we not perhaps live and love—that is, suffer and pity—in this all-enveloping Supreme Person—we, all the persons who suffer and pity and all the beings that strive to achieve personality, to acquire consciousness of their suffering and their limitation? And are we not, perhaps, ideas of this total Grand Consciousness, which by thinking of us as existing confers existence upon us? Does not our existence consist in being perceived and felt by God? And, further on, this same visionary tells us, under the form of images, that each angel, each society of angels, and the whole of heaven comprehensively surveyed, appear in human form, and in virtue of this human form the Lord rules them as one man.[3]

What is most surprising in all this is not that Unamuno cites Swedenborg, but rather the lucid exegesis that he makes of the Swede and the aptness of the citation. Clearing through the narrative entanglement of Swedenborg (his "form of images"), Unamuno has seen the essential, the substantive nucleus of Swedenborg's system: the vision of the world in personalized terms.[4] In fact, the paragraph in which the reference to Swedenborg was inserted belongs to a chapter (titled "Love, Suffering, Pity, and Personality") in which he debates the possibility of a personalized Universe. Few thinkers can exemplify this idea like Swedenborg, since in him we see neither a mysticism of the ineffable nor an indeterminate state of abyss in the Absolute, but rather the complete opposite. Swedenborg proposes a mysticism of the explainable, the determinable, and nameable.

This entire process for everything that can be explainable, determinable, and nameable is a step or a degree in the acquisition of consciousness and personality. In the language of Swedenborg: all this represents an angel, it becomes an angel.[5] Hence Unamuno's citation, because he has understood that the spirit of Swedenborg's writings is the maximum expression of a sphere of reality that has to be seen under personalized and personalizing categories. This also means, among other things, that reality is inserted into a context where determinations are qualitative and not quantitative. It is personalization that causes the unity of each consciousness (each angel, each determination) to be the parameter and paradigm by which the totality of all consciousness is measured.

Each consciousness is the All, and the All itself is a person. Swedenborg's vision has been correctly interpreted by Unamuno, and so he knew how to place that vision precisely where the problem of the personalization of the Universe arises. The category of person applied by Swedenborg to issues of a transcendental or metaphysical nature leads to a variety of ramifications and consequences, and Unamuno always kept this in mind. One of those corollaries is that the fundamental basis and representative character of Unamuno's system is the theme of personalization, which is also true of Swedenborg, since in Swedenborg's thought the same idea of person is *represented* by the figure of the angel. Unamuno knew how to capture the essence of Swedenborg's narratives. His thought typically values the concrete over the abstract and the image over the concept, since the personal (and personalizable) is always someone concrete, imaginable (it can refer to the image, to the figure), living, and existent. The determinations that fall under the ontological categories in Swedenborg—and that Unamuno rescues here—are not so much categories as living, existing *people:* this is the role of the angel in Swedenborg's thought. An ontology formulated in terms of the person is not an ontology of entities, ideas, or essences; it is an ontology of people with proper names, of concrete representations; in short, of existences. Unamuno was personally interested—in the full sense of the term—in the explanation of this conception, and this is clearly shown in another lucid citation of Swedenborg:

> If there is life in heaven there is change. Swedenborg remarked that the angels change, because the delight of the celestial life would gradually lose its value if they always enjoyed it in its fullness, and because angels, like men, love themselves, and he who loves himself experiences changes of state; and he adds further that at times the angels are

sad, and that he, Swedenborg, discoursed with some when they were sad (*Heaven and Hell,* §§158, 160).[6]

It would require a lengthy commentary to fully extract the meaning of this citation. We emphasize again the appropriateness of Unamuno's bringing up Swedenborg, because Unamuno saw how the theme of the angel responds to the motivations of existentialism that he himself promotes. The exegesis of the angel is nothing more than the phenomenalization of internal time as the movement and existence of the soul, the determination of a transcendental ontology characterized in personal, vital, concrete, and representable terms. In fact, the exegesis of the angel is one answer to the questions that Unamuno had just asked: "How can a human soul live and enjoy God eternally without losing its individual personality—that is to say, without losing itself? What is it to enjoy God? What is eternity as opposed to time? Does the soul change or does it not change in the other life? If it does not change, how does it live? And if it changes, how does it preserve its individuality through so vast a period of time?"[7]

These are the explicit referrals made by Unamuno in *The Tragic Sense of Life.* However, we believe that the Swedish thinker is present implicitly in other places in this work, and always in relation to the problem that we have pointed out. What Unamuno gleans from thinkers like Swedenborg is the dynamic, vital, and existential conception of the Transcendent, and the personalizing conception—with all its consequences—of both ontological and theological categories, with the known preeminence of the existential and concrete over the essentialist and abstract. This is why we say we can detect the presence of Swedenborg in the work of Unamuno in question. Do these words of Unamuno not have an evident Swedenborgian flavor? "May it not be, I say, that all souls grow without ceasing, some in a greater measure than others, but all having to pass some time through the same degree of growth, whatever that degree may be, and yet without ever arriving at the infinite, at God, to whom they continually approach?"[8]

Keeping in mind that we have extracted this citation from a context in which he is speaking of concepts such as apocatastasis and anacephalaeosis, this is obvious proof of Swedenborg's influence. Naturally, we don't mean to say that Swedenborg invented those terms or that Unamuno got them directly from him. Many authors, from Saint Paul on, have spoken of those concepts. However, it is the case that one of the conceptions that Unamuno picks, anacephalaeosis, is possible only in a personalizing system of the Universe and of all reality. It is possible only in a dynamic and existential vision of reality itself, one that thus continually receives its personalizing determinations—all of which is found in Swedenborg. Furthermore, we can classify Swedenborg within this line of thought because he has proposed in the West, in a discontinuous and diffuse manner, an ontology of figure and not concept, of person and not essence. This makes an examination of Swedenborg pertinent—and Unamuno saw this also. There are various passages in Unamuno's text, as we have stated, that we could link to Swedenborgian motifs. For example: "Heaven, then, so it is believed by many, is society, a more perfect society than that of this world; it is human society fused into a person. And there are not wanting some who believe that the tendency of all human progress is the conversion of our species into one collective being with real consciousness . . . and that when it shall have acquired full consciousness, all those who have existed will come to life again in it."[9]

Anyone who knows Swedenborg at all will read in these words a reference to the basic ideas of the Swedish thinker, and more specifically the above-mentioned vision of the society of angels as an overcoming of the quantitative by virtue of the preeminence of the personalizing and qualitative categories: "human society fused into a person," or, in other words, the All is repeated and determined in each one. One could argue that the preceding citation is found within a Pauline context, where we see a recurrence of the terms anacephalaeosis and apocatastasis, but it so happens that Swedenborg's thought is immersed in precisely that onto-theological tradition, and because of this we have both an explicit reference to him and an implicit embodiment of him in the text cited above.

We repeat once more, then, the central thread of our work: Unamuno has accomplished a perfect exegesis of Swedenborg, knowing how to see what was central and what was peripheral in him. We could also extend this exegesis of Unamuno to esoteric types of thought, for certainly it is no coincidence that authors such as Jacob Boehme and Friedrich Christoph Oetinger are also cited in the same text. This is tremendously symptomatic, especially in reference to Oetinger, since this theologian was the first translator of Swedenborg to German and his interpreter in Germany, which adds even more to our appraisal of Unamuno's interest in Swedenborg in particular and in esoteric thought in general. All this may lead us to think about the role that philosophy of a mystical-esoteric type has played in Unamuno. We are not trying to establish a direct line of influence between this philosophy and Unamuno, but undoubtedly our thinker knew of it and, more importantly, has been its lucid interpreter. If authors such as Boehme, Swedenborg, and Oetinger have been the object of study for Unamuno it is because all of them reveal a kind of mystical existentialism through which transcendental realities (God, the soul, supernatural life) are not resolved in abstract categories, but rather in personalized terms, or one might even say anthropomorphized. In any case, these mystical existentialisms assume a lived, concrete, and representable experience of those realities. This is one of Unamuno's deepest desires, one that could only be satisfied through the type of philosophy that we elsewhere called "mysticism of labeling."

As a final reflection in this small study, we need to once again mention Unamuno's hermeneutics with respect to Swedenborg. These hermeneutics have shown us how the thinker's profound meaning has appeared to us. We could then ask ourselves about the possible extension of those hermeneutics to all thought with those characteristics. In some ways this extension is already made by Unamuno himself with respect to Boehme and Oetinger, thus giving us a clue about Unamuno's religious influences, very distinct from the work that is usually cited (Saint Augustine, Spanish mysticism, Pascal, Kierkegaard) and with its complements. On the other hand, Unamuno proposes and carries out authentic hermeneutics that establish meaning. With Swedenborg, we have a telling example of this.

The Presence of Swedenborg in Eugeni d'Ors

It remains curious that although Emanuel Swedenborg was an author of such little resonance in the Hispanic culture, there have been among us two thinkers that have had a clear insight about the Swedish philosopher. We refer to Unamuno and to Eugeni d'Ors (1881–1954). We have already accounted for the former in the previous section. Let us then examine d'Ors. One of his earlier books, titled *Introducción a la vida angélica* (*Introduction to the Angelic Life*, 1939), has been reissued.[10] We already knew this book through the many references to it given by Henry Corbin. We cite the following two passages, which may be the most important:

> All these connections have been admirably presented in a small book with which we are far from being in total accord, but it is one toward which we want to show our generosity here, because it is one of the rare treatises of angelology written in our times and because a generous audacity inspires it at times.[11]

> I don't believe that one can find a better basis, simultaneously fundamental and experimental, to justify a small phrase written by a Catalonian writer of our times, in a treatise on angelology, written with a clairvoyant and resolved penetration, as a reply to a famous statement by Saint Teresa: No, it is not true that God alone suffices.[12]

There cannot be a better presenter for our theme than Henry Corbin, in that these citations serve as an entrance to this work: Swedenborg, the angel, d'Ors.

We will not attempt to demonstrate the influence of Swedenborg's angelology on that of d'Ors, but rather fundamentally show the understanding that d'Ors had of Swedenborg, which in an indirect fashion makes clear, in our judgment, the relevant role that Swedenborg played in the d'Orsian conception of the angel. However, Swedenborg's footprints on the philosophy of d'Ors are not limited purely to angelology, but also affect other topics. It is also true that the issue of the angel involves a variety of notional correlations, in such a way that they integrate into the global system, as we will see. We can say that the topic of the angel is emblematic, and it defines and represents a certain philosophy.

Now we examine the explicit references of d'Ors to Swedenborg. Xenius, his pseudonym, says: "I want to state clearly from the beginning that if I am to speak to you of Angels, it is with a very distinct spirit and tone from those present in the imagination, when one remembers Swedenborg or Dionysius the Areopagite . . . This apart from the fact that neither the Areopagite nor Swedenborg were what people imagine."[13]

First of all, it is noteworthy how for d'Ors Swedenborg is not a marginal, fantastical, or anecdotal author. He warns that Swedenborg is not what people imagine, undoubtedly making a reference to the multitude of misconceptions that are projected onto the Swedish thinker. Above all, it is very telling that d'Ors has placed Swedenborg in a book of angelology; it demonstrates not only a consideration of Swedenborg's importance on this topic, but also his presence in the body of d'Or's work, whether it be due to influence or due to a coincidence of the issues treated.

The second explicit reference to Swedenborg is the following:

> In commonplace judgment, Emmanuel Swedenborg, wise naturalist until a certain moment of his existence, begins to lose his mind at that moment and starts with his silliness concerning celestial things . . . Checking the dates, however, one notices how the author, who explains what he has seen and heard in heaven and hell, is simultaneously the creator of modern crystallography and he who discovers the connection of the sun and its system with the Milky Way. There is compatibility, then, between *Divine Love and Wisdom* and the most concrete scientific knowledge, and even with the practical discretion in the exercise of his technical functions and his political duties.[14]

In reality all of paragraph 30 is dedicated to Swedenborg, and in it we see the clarity of a rare intelligence that can size up the problematic issues always posed by the Scandinavian author. We see that d'Ors realizes that in Swedenborg there is no break between his scientific and spiritual work, but on the contrary Swedenborg's holistic vision consists precisely of extrapolating or extending scientific concepts (proper to the material world) to the world of the spirit, so reality presents itself as a continuum that, as d'Ors himself affirms, appears "compact, without cracks, without spaces." Few phrases could better define Swedenborg's system. There are not two Swedenborgs, one scientific and rational and another visionary and fanciful, and d'Ors knows this well. Contrary to what is often affirmed, there is no radical separation between the scientific Swedenborg and the theologian, simply because, we repeat, there has never been duality of thought, but rather continuity. Swedenborg's universe is one in which the structures of matter and the structures of spirit mutually correspond, and to explain this correspondence Swedenborg utilizes his scientific knowledge to extrapolate the spiritual sphere, applying a law of universal analogy. "Between the physical world and the spiritual world one must not imagine separation or hiatus," d'Ors states expressively. In this way Swedenborg reads the spiritual contents of the material world, its divine footprint, its symbol of the intelligible, and so he adds himself to the list of Christian exemplars in the history of philosophy. Another of the merits of d'Ors consists of conceiving of Swedenborg as an authentic philosopher and not just as a mystic.

What most interests us here is to confirm the penetrating interpretation that d'Ors develops of Swedenborg, versus the "commonplace judgment" that turns Swedenborg's speculations into a simple ecstatic trance. D'Ors shows himself to be an outstanding exegete of Swedenborg when he distinguishes between Swedenborg and his legion of Romantic followers, who often have presented a distorted vision of Swedenborg's thought.[15] We don't mean to minimize the role that Romanticism has played in the diffusion of Swedenborg's ideas; in any case, the echo of Swedenborg among Romantic writers is sociologically explainable. For us what matters is that d'Ors does not settle for preconceived ideas about Swedenborg, but rather has managed to read the profound meaning of the Swedish philosopher.

The d'Orsian understanding of Swedenborg is not centered on a global vision of the Nordic thinker; while the global vision may be accurate, in our judgment that understanding is given a concrete direction and explanation in the work of d'Ors. Naturally, we refer to angelology and, by extension, to the particular character that involves the figure of the angel in all thought systems where angels might be found. To stress the angelology of d'Ors is to stress all of his work, which is beyond our scope. But the influence of Swedenborg seems obvious in this theme in particular. The very fact that d'Ors dedicates to him a considerable space in a book on angelology proves it, since it isn't common that a thinker of the reputation and training of d'Ors would even consider Swedenborg. However, when studied in depth, the conceptions of d'Ors and Swedenborg coincide in many aspects. Fundamentally, they coincide in the ontology of determination, a determination that manifests as a rejection of the abstract and impersonal to affirm the figurative, the concrete, the personal—in a word, everything that is expressed in the image of the angel, the emblem and symbol of this class of philosophy, that is, of this theology of the namable. "God alone does not suffice"—that is, an abstract or apophatic notion of God does not suffice, but rather for us (who inhabit the images as our specific place) the angels mediate. They are the ones who approach us and represent that abstract and impersonal notion of the divine, which, though absolute, is not inapprehensible. Angels are the consequence of a theology of the namable and determinable (are not the angels the theophors of the divine names?), in which the absolute is made relative *for us.*

Without addressing the figure of the angel itself in d'Ors, a topic beyond our scope, we will nevertheless summarize the principal ways in which Swedenborg's presence can be perceived in the Spanish philosopher. First of all, there is the same consideration of the angel as a projection or a transcendental and spiritual dimension of human beings: to be human is to reach toward being an angel. Secondly, and as a corollary, is the concept of matrimony or syzygy of humans with their angels, that is, humans' obtaining the celestial part or dimension that is one's angel, which is expressed philosophically by saying that each angel is the unique form of each individual, his or her archetype or form. Thirdly, also closely related, is to note the similarity between the anthropological tripartite that is seen in both authors in relation to angelology: humans are natural, spiritual, and celestial for Swedenborg, and for d'Ors humans are composed of body, soul, and spirit or angel. In both cases the angel represents the personalization of human beings as they acquire their individual angels, which signifies the acquiring of true personality. In short, what identifies the d'Orsian and the Swedenborgian systems is their common interest in a figurative or emblematic thought in which conceptual categories become persons, in which universal emblems become symbols of *each person.* In each case the angel—symbol, genre, emblem—is presented as a being that directs every one of us. Metaphysically speaking, the principle of individualization of each one is his or her form, that is to say: it is *his* or *her* angel, the angel of *each* person.

However, it doesn't appear that the commentators who interpret d'Ors have been very responsive to Swedenborg's presence. None of the authors we have consulted even mention the Scandinavian philosopher. José Luis L. Aranguren, Díaz Plaja, Alain Guy, López Quintás, P. H. Michel, José Jiménez—none of them mention him, notwithstanding Jimenez's good prologue to his edition of *Introduction to the Angelic Life*. Of course this should be attributed not to the lack of awareness of d'Ors on the part of these authors, but rather the lack of comprehension of some aspects of Swedenborg.

Notwithstanding everything stated above, we cannot forget the differences that exist between our two thinkers. We see certain contradictions between the acceptance of some themes in Swedenborg by d'Ors and his system as a whole. The "classicism" of d'Ors prevented him from seeing that the development of Swedenborg's angelology led to the study of the Iranian world, which we appreciate in Corbin.[16] And in spite of everything we need to emphasize the interest in Swedenborg that has arisen as much in d'Ors as in Unamuno. This interest is one that is undoubtedly justified by the type of spiritualistic existentialism, metaphysical individualism, and personalism that characterize Swedenborg's thought, qualities that also serve as a vital intellectual bedrock for the two Spanish philosophers, no matter how they differ from each other. It is in this sense that we affirm that d'Ors has been a profound exegete of Swedenborg's work: for him—as for Unamuno—Swedenborg is primarily a thinker concerned with the person, the concrete, the individual (and is the angel not the figure the represents these characteristics on the highest level?). In fact, what d'Ors and Swedenborg have in common is what we could call an emblematic philosophy, philosophy that is synthesized in this d'Orsian phrase: "The eon is an idea with a biography."

Swedenborg and the Religiosity of Jorge Luis Borges

Very possibly Jorge Luis Borges is the Spanish-language author who has engaged Swedenborg the most. This fact is in and of itself worthy of consideration. But this relationship raises another theme: the connection that may exist between philosophy and literature. In the specific case of Swedenborg and Borges, the problem poses itself in the following manner: What does the Argentine contribute to our understanding of the Swede? And to what extent does Swedenborg's work illuminate the work of Borges?

In principle, the repeated citations of Swedenborg in Borges shouldn't surprise us much, given that Borges is a writer who makes frequent use of philosophers (Plato, Spinoza, Schopenhauer, etc.) and given that Swedenborg has been an influential thinker, especially with the cultured. Without attempting an exhaustive inventory of all the references Borges makes to the Prophet of the North, we will expound the clearest and most important ones, since those will tell us what interested Borges about Swedenborg, and possibly also what the Argentinean could add to our knowledge of the Swedish theologian.

There are two texts in which Borges examines a type of Swedenborgian doctrinal synthesis: one of those is a prologue to an English-language volume about Swedenborg;[17] the other, which is practically identical to the first one, only abbreviated, is the text of a paper given at the University of Belgrano in 1978 and collected in the volume *Borges Oral*.[18] These summaries, in spite of a few inevitable inaccuracies due to their brevity, are well constructed and in addition give us a complete idea of what could most have interested Borges about Swedenborg: it was above all the lucidity of the Swedish visionary, in spite of all the clichés and accusations of insanity. Borges's verification of Swedenborg's lucidity means, first of all, an entry point for any approach to Swedenborg (the fact that he has something to say makes subsequent exploration possible); and secondly, the necessity of a certain interpretation of the writings of Swedenborg: that a correct understanding of the Scandinavian is not possible without *ad hoc* hermeneutics. In addition, there are several interesting notes that Borges has detected in the wise Nordic, such as the mention of the formal, concrete, and individual character of the supersensible worlds. But above all we are interested in the factors that affect what we could call the religiosity of Borges: "According to Swedenborg, hell and heaven are in human beings, which likewise include planets, mountains, seas, continents, minerals, trees, herbs, flowers, thistles, caltrops, animals, reptiles, birds, fish, tools, cities, and buildings."[19] Here we may have the key for Borges's attraction to Swedenborg: the internalizing of spheres and categories normally projected *ad extra*. The work (and the religiosity) of Swedenborg would then be a process through which the soul lives in its interior what others place outside. All those planets, mountains, and so on are now movements, flows, transformations, and explanations of the consciousness. It is in the soul that all those places reside, since they are events of the soul—that is, they are what lives in the soul. In the impressive sonnet that Borges dedicates to Swedenborg the same idea is expressed:

> *He knew that heaven and hell*
> *and their mythologies are in your soul.*[20]

What Borges has intuited in Swedenborg's works is what Henry Corbin has developed *in extenso:* a phenomenology of the visionary consciousness, where the journeys, the epics, and the worlds described with picturesque color are metaphors and images of spiritual realities.[21] Borges's reading of Swedenborg is in certain measure comparable to the one made by Strindberg, who wrote, "The reading of Swedenborg occupies all my day; the realism of his descriptions overwhelms me. Everything is found in them, all my observations, my sensations, my ideas, in such a way that his visions seem vivid to me, as authentic human documents. It isn't exactly believing blindly; it is enough to read and compare with one's own lived experiences."[22] In Strindberg the parallelism between Swedenborg's internalization and his own is more existential.

For Strindberg as well as for Borges, Swedenborg's heaven and hell are internalizations of the consciousness that lives in heaven or hell. That is, each person is his or her own heaven or hell. Heaven and hell are thus representations of inner experiences, in the same way that the dwellings of Saint Teresa or the castles of Sohravardi represent processes and events of inwardness and its states.

Another reference to Swedenborg by the Hispanic writer centers on the latter's interest in what we could call inner religiosity or internalizing of religious images and figures: "For Swedenborg, as with Boehme, heaven and hell are states that humans freely seek, not a pious or penal establishment."[23] Possibly the consequences that Borges could extract from this interpretation of Swedenborg were as much of an aesthetic nature as of philosophical or spiritual; aesthetics, because of the latent possibilities that assume the assertion of the preeminence of inwardness; and philosophical or spiritual, because of the special mode of religiosity that inner experience involves. Perhaps it would be excessive to include Borges within what we might call Swedenborgian spirituality, but it is indisputable that Borges felt more than just a culturalist or name-dropping attraction to Swedenborg.[24] Borges suspected that what Swedenborg tells us refers, above all, to realities of the soul. In light of this, the Buddha of the North would come to propose an internalized spirituality, and to some degree a demythologized religiosity, in which images and representations are resolved in experiences of the soul. This demythologizing aspect of Swedenborg's hermeneutics, an essential characteristic of every allegorical exegesis, was clearly noticed by Borges, who has caught sight of the fundamental idea that underlies the thought of the Scandinavian visionary. Consequently, if for Unamuno Swedenborg would be a type of precursor of the philosophy of existence, and if for d'Ors a theoretician of angelology, Borges would highlight Swedenborg as a thinker of the interiority of consciousness.

Undoubtedly there are enormous possibilities for developing the philosophical and theological consequences of this Swedenborgian conceptualization. However, we have stated that Borges remains in an intuitive phase with these ideas, and furthermore we need to keep in mind that Borges is not a Swedenborgian in any strict sense, nor is he a philosopher or theologian, and so consequently we shouldn't expect a complete and detailed exposition of the Swede's theories. Yet the interest that Swedenborg arouses in Borges is clearly evident. Proof of this are the six inclusions of Swedenborg's writings (more than any other author) in *El libro del cielo y del infierno* (*The Book of Heaven and Hell*),[25] in addition to another text by Heine that includes an interesting reflection on Swedenborg. The Heine reference can be placed within the line that sees the Prophet of the North as a thinker in which concrete individuality, internalization of consciousness, and the impulse toward form take precedence above all else. In similar fashion, in *Cuentos breves y extraordinarios* (*Extraordinary Tales*) we find another reference to Swedenborg.[26] Finally, in "Otro poema de los dones" ("Another Poem of the Gifts") we find a general recognition of his figure: "For Sweden-borg, who conversed with the angels in the streets of London."[27]

In short, we believe that Swedenborg inspires Borges to experience religiosity in a certain way. We leave the word "religiosity" in all its ambivalence, because it is not clear that the Argentine author ever affirmed a definite religion. However, it does seem evident that he participated in the feelings and experiences of authentic religiosity. In these sentiments and experiences Swedenborg's role is noteworthy: the process of internalization, the demythologizing exegesis, the spiritualization of categories formulated in *ad extra* projection, religious life in relation to spontaneity of consciousness, and so on. Swedenborg's footprints lie in all these expressions of the soul's activities. If the influence of a certain spirituality in Borges is important, however, equally important is the fact that Borges knew how to interpret and extract such intelligent notes from an author like Swedenborg, who has not often enjoyed such lucid readings. What matters here is not just what Swedenborg's work has been able to contribute to Borges, but also what illumination Borges has been able to contribute to a better comprehension of the wise Swede. Hence, if Swedenborg's presence can help us to better understand not only the literature but the innermost religiosity of Borges, certainly Borges's intuitions permit us to contribute data when the interpretation is of an author so often misunderstood as is Swedenborg.

We have not noted any other allusion to the importance of Swedenborg in Borges's books. Or perhaps we have, indirectly, in an implicit way. We are speaking of a beautiful poem of undoubtedly Swedenborgian resonance that carries the significant title of "The Angel" and ends with:

> Lord, at the end of my life on Earth
> I do not dishonor the Angel.[28]

In the literature of Borges there is a key citation that truly signals a landmark for establishing the author's spiritual affiliation. This sign or symptom is Gustav Theodor Fechner. It is not our intention to draw conclusions from or exaggerate the importance of this reference, but rather to point out possible indicators of this attitude. It is in this vein that we cite Fechner, and more specifically *The Book of Heaven and Hell*, page 142 (we refer to Fechner's text "Extensions," extracted from his peculiar *Zend-Avesta*). "Extensions," the text selected by Borges and by Bioy Casares, in our judgment enters headlong into this tendency, characteristic of an internalist religiosity, in which theologoumenon and mythologem are resolved in movements and states of the soul, a religiosity that in Borges connects with Swedenborgian motifs. Following the terminology used above, the cited paragraph by Fechner is an example of what could be called a Swedenborgian spiritual affiliation. In addition, Fechner presents us with a kind of *tertium comparationis* in another author also cited previously and for whom likewise Swedenborg occupied an important role: Henry Corbin. In effect, in Corbin's book *Corps spirituel et Terre celeste (Spiritual Body and Celestial Earth)*, Fechner is cited at length in relation to a very typically Swedenborgian topic, the angel. A system of cross-references would place us in the same sequence from Corbin, Swedenborg, and Fechner to Borges, and to all possible combinations among those authors.

As a consequence, when it comes time to explain the religiosity of Borges, the mediation of Fechner with Borges reveals an additional characteristic of this spirituality, one that occurs in a special way: the life of consciousness and its explanation.

Primordial Language and Pure Poetry (Aspects Common to Swedenborg and Juan Ramón Jiménez)

With this brief piece we want to show how certain philosophical-religious conceptions have been able to influence—directly or indirectly—a field that may seem distinct and distant from our topic. Specifically, we want to show how the idea of angelic language—the original language—is present in the genesis and development of Juan Ramón Jiménez's idea of pure poetry. Indeed, we can see the operation of a theological paradigm in some of his determinations.

There are two ways to confirm Swedenborg's presence in the work and thought of Juan Ramón Jiménez. One is to look for direct references the Spanish poet has made to the Swedish theologian. The other is to phenomenologically analyze themes in the poet's work that are similar to those made by Swedenborg. With respect to the first, only one explicit citation of Swedenborg can be found in the books of Juan Ramón Jiménez. It is from *Jardines lejanos (Distant Gardens)* where he writes:

> *But it is your white light, moon*
> *Peace, oblivion made of love,*
> *Light that had the fortune*
> *Of reaching Swedenborg*[29]

This is a typically symbolist vision of Swedenborg with Romantic echoes.[30] The mention of Swedenborg contributes, furthermore, to the creation of an evocative and suggestive atmosphere, reflecting the idea that the symbolist had of the wise Swede. Swedenborg's theory of correspondences and representations is no longer interpreted in a transcendent way, but rather by relating sensations, memories, and evocations to their correlates in the present world (and not in the transcendent world, as did the Swedenborgian Romantics). In short, for Juan Ramón Jiménez (as for the symbolist interpretation), correspondences are horizontal and not vertical, and within that horizontality one finds the figure of Swedenborg as a source of synesthesia.

However, there is another way of relating Juan Ramón to Swedenborg: the one we referred to at the beginning, which consists of approaching the two authors in terms of a similar treatment of themes. To be specific, the argument we will follow now will be the connection between the idea of pure poetry and that of the original language in Swedenborg. The notion of a primordial language of humanity is, as we know, a recurrent theme in the history of conceptions of language (and one that certainly acquires a great vitality in Romanticism). This original language, or Adamic language, would designate the exact name of things and would thus provide a vital contact with the thing named, since in fact a fundamental quality of the language would be the establishment of a direct relationship between the word and the thing of which one is speaking. This is an old and mythic conception, one that claims that the mother language would be essential and actually motivated by its naming function. Hence the sacred connotation of that language, since in some ways it would coincide with the pristine divine revelation. That primordial language would be, then, the language of the dawn of humanity, one that would show the most immediate communication between God and humans. This comes close to the issue of definitively identifying the original and primordial language, whether it be Hebrew, Sanskrit, etc. We should also make the connection to the Romantic consideration of poetry as a vestige or derivation of the original language, together with the conglomeration of stories, legends, and popular stories that laography (folklore) describes to us.[31]

Swedenborg called this language the language of the angels, which was, furthermore, the language that the Most Ancient Church spoke; according to Swedenborg, at that time antediluvian humanity lived in a state of pristine openness toward the divine (and hence spoke the language of angels). In *Heaven and Hell*, Swedenborg says: "I have been told that the first language of people on our earth shared this nature because it was given them from heaven, and that Hebrew resembles it in some respects" (§237). And later in the same work: "I have been told that before letters were invented, the earliest humans on our planet had this kind of writing, and that it was transferred into Hebrew letters" (§260).

In the exegetical plane, the language of the angels refers to the most profound meaning of Scripture, that which the angels know directly without any type of mediation. For this type of theological-linguistic ideology, the Bible acquires the role of fundamental and privileged vestige of the primordial language.

> As for the Word in heaven, it is written in a spiritual style that is completely different from an earthly style. A spiritual style consists of nothing but letters, each one of which enfolds a meaning. There are also marks over the letters that highlight the meaning.
>
> For angels of the spiritual kingdom the letters look like typeset letters in our world; and the letters for angels of the heavenly kingdom—each of which enfolds a whole meaning—are like the ancient Hebrew letters, various curved, with marks over and within them.
>
> Since this is what their writing is like, there are no personal or place names in their Word as there are in ours. Instead of the names there are the realities of what they mean. (*Sacred Scripture* §71)[32]

Since this language (and consequently this form of biblical inter-pretation) is the most original, it also consequently corresponds to the oldest form of humanity (or to the state of consciousness—the eon—that could represent the image of Adamic humanity).

Romanticism's interest in pristine forms of expression, with their el-ements of original revelation, being the source of all subsequent nar-rative and linguistic modes, is reflected in the great quantity of intel-lectual figures who are interested in and who study the topic.[33] The clarification of the original language involved the clarification of the original revelation itself, since it is evident that they were identified with each other. From there, as we have stated, all the traditional and popular narratives were derived, and poetry itself managed to gain the status of first language of the human race. The importance given to the primordial language resided in what its speech implied for human be-ings. To retain that mythic language meant to be open to the essential reality of things, and so things were open to human comprehension (upon being named, that is). By means of the primordial language hu-mans name essentially, that is, they enter into direct communication with the intimate essence of reality: they name things as they are, and thus provide the motive for language. It is the *lingua volucris* (language of the birds) of so many legends—reflected also in mythemes such as the one in which pre-Fall humanity could speak with the animals. All of these are metaphors for the radical ontological transparency of the world that, with respect to human beings, denotes that linguistic com-munication. Above all, the primordial language would be the mytho-poetic expression by which Meaning makes itself present to humans by means of things, and humans open themselves to the establishment and reception of this Meaning. The primordial language, poetry itself, is revelation; and hence the connection of this theme with the Bible, traditional myths and legends, etc. They are footprints, indications of the primordial language of humanity.

Related to these speculations are references to the deepest sense of the kabbalah, and the very presence of it in authors who are concerned with language in its transcendental dimension, since the essence of the kabbalah consists of explaining language as universal human partici-pation in the emergence of Meaning that is manifested through logophany. The kabbalah as a tradition *(parádosis)* means the constant animating of meaning, which is maintained as such through the living community that continuously updates it. Thus, the kabbalah is restoration of meaning, fulfilled eschatology of meaning. In this way, the kabbalah becomes a paradigm of all hermeneutics, and at the same time manifests the genetic and systematic relationship between itself, biblical exegesis, and the issue of the origin of language (of course, the primitive language is retained by the kabbalah). Hamann could already see these connections when referring to *Aestetica in Nuce* as a "rhapsody in kabbalistic prose."

As we have stated, in the specific case of Swedenborg the name that this primordial language takes is the language of the angels. What the wise Swede does is take all the qualities that other authors have attributed to the primordial universal language (which in turn is a figure that represents language as transcendent) and attribute them to angelic language. This is perfectly in keeping with the rest of Swedenborg's system, because if everything angelic signifies human fullness, we conclude that the language of the angels is human language in its fullest aspect. An indication of this is the fact that the angelic language encompasses the inner sense of the Bible directly, without symbolic mediation, since both coincide. In effect—and this clearly demonstrates the exegetic element of Swedenborg's thought—the language of the angels represents the *actual* sense of the Bible, that is, the restorative hermeneutics that causes the meaning to be present. It is also consequential that the humanity of the Adamic state—the Most Ancient Church, the people that lived closest to God—has the language closest to the language of the angels, and therefore can penetrate into the innermost levels of biblical meaning: "The earliest people, who lived before the flood and whose era was called the Golden Age, had direct revelation and therefore had divine truth written on their hearts" (*White Horse* §6).[34] In short, this language of the angels (for Swedenborg, the primordial and ideal language), this immediate, unmediated revelation is what reveals the inner nature of the speaker—language that is pure spontaneity of consciousness. The words of this language are simple, direct, intuitive, universal, and display the internal qualities of the one who speaks—it is a language, then, that is identified with consciousness. "The reason [all spirits speak in their own language] is that the language that spirits are familiar with is composed not of words but of thoughts. This language is common to all tongues" (*Secrets of Heaven* §1637). This would be, in the context of the Islamic-Iranian philosophy, the language *yabaruti*.

A universal language—a language that directly demonstrates meaning itself (paradigmatically, the biblical meaning) as much as the immediacy of the inner nature of the subject—acquired in Swedenborg the characteristic of a *mathesis universalis* (universal learning). This was reflected in his *Hieroglyphic Key,* a concrete embodiment of what for him should have been a retained language, one of the closest possible to the angelic language.[35]

Our thesis rests on establishing a relationship between the concept of primordial or angelic language and the concept of pure poetry in Juan Ramón Jiménez, a relationship that would be both phenomenological and historical, as we stated earlier.

According to Blasco,[36] the influence of Swedenborg on Juan Ramón Jiménez is noteworthy in that it respects the significance of the awareness of the poet from Moguer, a significance that begins to clarify itself after *Eternidades (Eternities),* that is, after what we could call the metaphysical Juan Ramón Jiménez. Just after *Eternidades* begins, and undoubtedly in relation to the idea of consciousness, nature takes center stage in Juan Ramón with the idea of poetic language as the true words for things, that is, the notion of pure poetry. Historically speaking, there is a common thread that connects speculations about universal language with ideas about poetry as reconstruction or construction (as the case may be) of that pristine language. In effect, we consider that behind the category of pure poetry there are underlying Romantic theories of poetry as mythic, Adamic language. In fact, for the Romantics, poetry was what remained and what we could recover of that primordial language, whether by the inspiration of the poets, or what one could find through investigation of popular forms, or in the body of material composed of legends, stories, and traditional narratives (fairy tales, romances, etc.). Later, after symbolism and Stéphane Mallarmé, it was no longer a matter of recovering primordial language and essence, it was a matter of recreating it: it is undoubtedly a demystified vision of the theme. Juan Ramón owes much to the latter, but also we consider that our poet has a metaphysical impulse to recover in some form the essential words for things. That is to say, he seeks the experience of the fundamental opening of reality that provides the exact name for things: the experience of the Logos, in fact.

My eternal word!
Oh, what supreme living
In nothingness the language of my mouth
(Eternidades, 137)

I would like my book to be,
As are the heavens at night,
All present truth, without history
(Piedra y Cielo [Stone and Sky], 119)[37]

However, it is above all the phenomenological relationship that makes it possible to compare the concept of the language of the angels in Swedenborg and the idea of pure poetry in Juan Ramón Jiménez. Would the Spanish poet not happily affirm the following definition of pure poetry offered by the Swedish visionary regarding the language of angels?

[The angels] can in a single word express what we cannot say in a thousand words. (*Heaven and Hell* §239)

Because angels' language flows directly from their affection . . . angels can express in a minute more than we can say in half an hour, and can present in a few words things that would make many pages of writing. (*Heaven and Hell* §240)[38]

There is a certain concord in angelic speech that is indescribable. This concord stems from the fact that the thoughts and affections that give rise to speech flow forth and spread out in keeping with heaven's form, heaven's form being what determines how everyone there associates and communicates. (*Heaven and Hell* §242)

Angelic speech presents an image of heaven's structure. All angelic speech therefore exhibits songlike harmony ending in a single syllable. . . . The reason this happens, I was told, is that everything in heaven harks back to the one God as its one end in view. This evidence too showed me that all thought and therefore all speech flows in from the Lord through heaven, which is the source of this harmony in speech that ends in a unified cadence. (*Secrets of Heaven* §7191)

This relationship that Swedenborg establishes between finality and unity as characteristics of angelic language (that is, the original or ideal language) is interesting: "Angels speak in terms of purpose and therefore usefulness, which are the first and most important elements of any subject" (*Secrets of Heaven* §1645).[39]

According to the internal logic of Swedenborg's system, if the angelic dimension represents the fullness of humanity, then the language of the angels means the full human language, as we stated earlier. In addition, according to the internal logic of the same system, the fullness of the language involves its reduction to consciousness, to interiority, which is in fact what Swedenborg does when he describes his celestial language. It is pure movement of consciousness: intuitive, direct, simple, instantaneous, interior, motivated.

These factors described bear directly on Juan Ramón Jiménez's idea of pure poetry. The essential language in Swedenborg's version is molded to the fundamental characteristics of our poet, since, ultimately, pure poetry represents the new flowering of the old idea of a language that makes the innermost reality of things present:[40]

> *Where is the word, heart*
> *That beautifies with love the ugly world,*
> *That gives it forever—and only already—*
> *Strength of a child*
> *And defense of a rose?*
> (Belleza [Beauty], 86)

In addition, for Juan Ramón Jiménez the binomial of primordial language and pure poetry acquires a dimension of consciousness. It is pure consciousness to the degree in which it establishes direct communication between the poet, the world, and human beings, that is, the spontaneity of an experience in dealing with reality. That is what expresses the commonality between naming and consciousness, and that is what makes possible the identification of pure poetry as the essential words for things:

Of all the white and black secrets,
Coincides to him in echo, enamored,
Full and tall of all its treasures,
The profound, silent, true word
That only he has heard, he will hear in his vigilance.
The flesh, the soul one of him, in its air,
Only then word:
Beginning and end,
Present with no more turning of a head,
Destiny, flame, odor, rock, wing, legitimate,
Life and death,
Nothingness or eternity: then word.
(La estación total [The Entire Season], 14)

These poems that we have cited close a book or a poetic cycle, and as a kind of conclusion assume a reflection of the ultimate subject and the object of the poetic composition: the poetic word itself that, in a circular process, makes the poem possible and itself culminates with the very creation of the poem. We are dealing with a reduction or assimilation of being with language and consciousness, and consequently the consideration of the poet as demiurge, or participant at least in that demiurgic reality. Having arrived at this point, we must address the arduous and much-debated issue of the possible mysticism or pantheism of Juan Ramón Jiménez, although obviously we cannot fully address this problem here. We maintain only that language and consciousness form a substantive part of a hypothetical mystical or religious vision of Juan Ramón, and they are in this way essential pieces for becoming familiar with this aspect that is so important to the work and life of our author. We claim, however, that for Juan Ramón Jiménez the essential language of things, the pure poetry, is conceived more than anything as a construction of the poet himself, thus placing himself in an allegiance with Mallarmé, as is indicated in these verses:

"To a poet
(for an unwritten book)"

We believe the names.
They will derive men

Later they will derive things.
And only the world of names will remain,
Words of love for humans,
Of odor of the roses.
Of love and the roses
Only the names must remain.
We believe the names.

(Poemas impersonales. Leyenda [Impersonal Poems: Legend], 42)

Phenomenologically speaking, primordial language, angelic language, and pure poetry can be placed on the same scale or representative sequence: they all refer to a similar experience of meaning. Historically, the sphere in which the conception of pure poetry—of all contemporary poetry, according to some—emerges is indebted to those speculations about a primordial and universal language, whether or not it be fixed in a particular language.

All in all, for Swedenborg pristine language signifies collaboration with the spontaneous movement of consciousness. In an analogous way, to speak of universal consciousness assumes also, and in an inescapable manner, that one is speaking of pure poetry and a language of that universal consciousness, if not an identification between the two. In this sense we consider Juan Ramón Jiménez as a continuance of the problem revived and developed by, among others, Emanuel Swedenborg. We can, then, trace a line of continuity, as much from a phenomenological aspect as a historical one, among categories such as primordial language, angelic language, and *mathesis universalis,* all manifested in Swedenborg. We would insert the pure poetry of Jiménez into this same alliance because of its transformation, development, or echo of those same categories. So, pure poetry as *mathesis universalis?* That could well be the profound sense of the verse from Jiménez: "The name drawn from the names" (*Dios deseado y deseante [God Desired and Desiring],* 2).

Swedenborg in Maria Zambrano

We will now briefly examine the figure of Maria Zambrano.[41] There are sufficient elements in her work to justify the fact that she might have felt attracted to the Swedish mystic. In fact, trying to reconcile conceptual and representative thought with rationality and spirituality is a constant in Zambrano. From this perspective one cannot speak only of her study under José Ortega y Gasset and Javier Zubiri; we need to speak also of Miguel de Unamuno, as she herself recognizes. Later she would have dialogs with Octavio Paz, Henry Corbin, Elemire Zolla, and other figures from the Eranos group, figures that we could consider to be favorable for knowledge of Swedenborg.

The general platform of Zambrano's philosophy, as stated earlier, approaches issues related to Swedenborg's platform, and what stands out the most is the search for the original Word as reconciliation of the dualities cited earlier. For Zambrano, pure poetry becomes an emblematic paradigm of primordial and sacred language, a common source of Logos and myth, of concept and narrative. Hence the interest of Maria Zambrano in Saint John of the Cross, in the later Heidegger, and, naturally, also in Emanuel Swedenborg. Some titles of her works are very significant: *Apuntes sobre el lenguaje sagrado y los artes (Notes on Sacred Language and the Arts), Filosofía y poesía (Philosophy and Poetry), De la Aurora (Of the Aurora), Claros del bosque (Clearings in the Forest),* and so on. It is also significant that this thinker from Málaga possessed a copy of a work by Swedenborg in her private library, whose Spanish title is *La Vida Espiritual y la Palabra Sagrada (Spiritual Life and the Sacred Word;* this volume is an anthology of the work published in English as *Apocalypse Explained*).[42] We shall now proceed to give some concrete testimonies to Swedenborg's presence in Maria Zambrano.

In *Delirio y destino (Delirium and Destiny),* a memoir, we find the first reference to the Nordic: "Fervent and objective historian of the heterodoxies [referring to the erudite Menéndez Pelayo, author of *History of Spanish Heterodoxies*], of all of the heterodoxies in Spain, from Prisciliano, until the same day he died in 1912, so that he was unable to name the Church of Sudenborg [sic], established with unknown continuity in Valencia in the following year."

In a personal letter to the philosopher and theologian Agustín Andreu, in October of 1974, she affirms:

Walking between the shelves [of the University of Madrid Library] a person came by to greet me and I rested my left hand over the row of books. Later I looked to see what book I had my hand on, and I read:

De las maravillas del cielo y del infierno [Heaven and Hell], bound edition, perfect printing of 1913, New York, in Spanish that later amazed
me for being from the seventeenth century, in the style of a "Guide"
[referring to the *Guía de pecadores (The Sinner's Guide)* of Louis of
Granada] . . . I took it home. On the inside cover it had a seal of ink
that said: Association for the promotion of the New Church. Valencia,
55 Alameda Street.

A bit later she tells about going to Valencia and finding the house
at 55 Alameda, which was the headquarters of the Swedenborg Association of Spain and the family residence of its founder, the Norwegian
Jörgen Hartvig Andersen. She adds: "It would be interesting to know
something about the success of Swedenborg and his angels in Spain,
besides the not-very-interesting articles of don Eugenio."[43] It doesn't
seem like she was very sympathetic toward d'Ors.

In another of Zambrano's important books we find the following
reference: "Speaking of angels, Swedenborg says that when they ascend
to a plane higher than what is natural for them, they feel anguished."
We can compare this idea with another paragraph taken from the letter
alluded to earlier (when she referred to *Heaven and Hell*): "I remember
only this marvel—there were many—that the Angels that travel according to their species in a specific zone with freedom to go to another
zone; when they ascend they feel anguish, and when they descend they
feel desperation. Doesn't this same thing happen to us humans?"

Maria Zambrano—as with Strindberg, another great Swedenborgian—posits the necessity of a descent to the inner parts of oneself
(*descensus ad inferos,* dark night of the soul) in order to obtain a vital
and regenerative knowledge. And she sees in the life of Swedenborg's
angels a metaphorical prefiguring of our own existential experience,
something Swedenborg actually thought himself. It is noteworthy that
Maria Zambrano, hardly knowing the work of the Swede, had intuited
its existential stamp.

To conclude this brief reference to Maria Zambrano we will allude
one more time to the primordial Word and to poetry as a desire for rescue of the lost language:

And from where this irresistible desire surges, born of nostalgia
revived by hope, of having lost it, that if in any art there is a privileged

reflection, it is in poetry . . . The sacred word is active, operational, word-action without needing to be imperative . . . All poetry will have or will seek to have, and in the saddest cases try ineffectually to have, something of this sacred autonomous language . . . In eminent places of philosophical thought, when rigor fully shines in the definitions, theorems, and principles, there appears a type of sacred language. (*Apuntes sobre el lenguaje sagrado y los artes*)

After reading those fragments, can we not evoke one more time Swedenborg's ideas on the language of angels or on the most pristine sense of the Bible? That is why Alicia Sánchez Dorado has been able to compare, in a forthcoming work on the two authors we are examining, those two texts, revealing their similarity. The text of Zambrano says, in reference to the sacred language in liturgy: "The participation of the body—movements of transposition that stop being simply transpositions, simply walking, circumambulation, dance—fulfill the action of the sacred word. And all this, far from constituting an invasion of the corporeal in the area of the word, denotes the submission of the body, a submission that rescues it from its isolation, from its sad and tiring autonomy, of its being only an instrument of work or of pleasure" (*Apuntes sobre el lenguaje sagrado y los artes*). In a comparable text by Swedenborg it is stated this way:

It can be said of all regenerated people that they are their own truth and their own good, since truth is the origin of the thinking that arises from their understanding, and good is the origin of the feelings that arise from their will. . . . The body only does what it is told; that is, it speaks the thoughts that arise from our understanding and it acts on the feelings that arise from the will. In this way thinking and willing correspond with the body, and the body with them; and they form a unity with it, like an effect and the cause of that effect. And all these taken together are what constitute a human being. (*Apocalypse Explained* §1071)[44]

In summary, Unamuno finds in Swedenborg a model of expression of the existential consciousness and of his experiences; d'Ors postulates the spiritual configuration of the person by means of the image of the angel; Jiménez and Zambrano are interested in Swedenborg's conception of the primordial Word and Scripture and the possibilities they entail. It should be emphasized again that Swedenborg's concept of language served as a rich source for authors such as Zambrano. Heidegger is not the only one with foundational speculations about primordial language and poetry; the Swede has also contributed profound arguments to the metaphysical reflection concerning language. Mystical existentialism and pristine language: here we see the contributions of Maria Zambrano to the understanding of Swedenborg.

History of the Swedenborg Society in Spain

On other occasions I have referred to the scant audience for Swedenborgian ideas in Spain.[45] It seems to me of special interest to trace the history of the Swedenborg Society of Spain, since surely it represents the most serious attempt (but in vain, as we shall see) to spread Swedenborg's doctrine among Spaniards.[46] The Swedenborg Society of Spain was founded in Valencia during the first decade of the twentieth century by the Norwegian citizen Jörgen Hartvig Andersen. Let us proceed step by step, beginning with a brief sketch of Andersen.

Jörgen Hartvig Andersen was born November 9, 1861, in Sarpsborg (Norway, though at that time the nation belonged to Sweden). He was the son of Hans Christensen and Ingeborg Karine Hansen, the sixth of fourteen children. He abandoned his homeland at a young age to work overseas, always in the business of maritime transportation. On January 21, 1881, he boarded the fishing vessel *Angelo* to the city of Hull and then on to Leith (both cities in England), where he joined the business of Sm. C. Miller & Co., living in various boarding houses. Later he worked as managing director in the subsidiary of Rayner & Möller (owned by a Norwegian) in West Hartlepool (the home office was in Sunderland, also England). In August 1885 he enlisted in the military in the Smaalenes Batallion in Fredrikstad, Norway, later to depart to Cherbourg, France, where he worked in the shipping company of A. Langlois & E. Buhot. Just before Christmas 1888 he went to Valencia, where he worked for the Hilario lumber company. In 1889 he began to work with the Dane Halfdan Enberg, with whom he founded the firm Enberg & Co. In 1882 he met Sigrid Wilhelmina Larson (1871–1950), of Swedish nationality, on board the steamship *Sitona* (the owner being

Jörgen's brother Karl) on a trip from Sweden to London. On June 3, 1895, they married in the British capital. The document that certifies the marriage was signed by the *legationspredikant* (pastor of the Swedish Lutheran Church, ascribed to the Swedish official) of the Swedish Church in London, the same church where Swedenborg's remains were buried until they were moved to Uppsala, Sweden, in 1908. The newlyweds moved to Skällebred (in Sweden, the ancestral home of Sigrid's parents), only later to move to Valencia (Colón Street, and later Alameda Avenue) where both would reside (with a brief break during the Spanish Civil War) until their retirement to Denia (Alicate), where they died.

Sigrid was a cultured woman interested in all types of knowledge. They had five children: Astrid Karin Mercedes (translator into Norwegian of *Platero y yo [Platero and I]* by Juan Ramón Jiménez); Raghild Anna Conchita, who compiled and organized all the documentation that referred to her father; Sigrid Thora Emilia and Ingrid Mercedes, the latter a painter, and the only daughters that outlived their father; and Ingar Karl August, who died at age forty-three of lung cancer.

Settled in Valencia, Andersen managed a ship consignment business. Starting in 1922 he served as the Norwegian vice consul, and shortly thereafter as honorary consul (1930). In 1929 he received the Norwegian State Order of Saint Olaf in recognition of this work. At the outbreak of the Spanish Civil War in 1936, Andersen and his family sought refuge in Norway, where in 1937 he suffered a stroke. At the end of the war in 1939 he returned to Valencia and lived there until his death in 1946 (in Villa Conchita, his house in the coastal city of Denia). Curiously, one month later Halfdan Enberg, Andersen's former partner and at that time the Danish consul, died in Barcelona.

J. H. Andersen's discovery of Swedenborg's ideas and his unconditional conversion to them occurred in Valencia, where he met a Mrs. Mertens from the United States. She, her husband, and their three children were neighbors of the Andersen family on 55 Alameda Avenue (the address to which Maria Zambrano referred; this would be the official address of the Swedenborg Society of Spain and of the *Heraldo de la Nueva Iglesia [Herald of the New Church]*). The first contact with the Mertenses was on Christmas 1889, and we can set the year 1900 as the date of J. H. Andersen's conversion to Swedenborgianism. His ascendance and contact with Swedenborgianism at the international level, and more specifically with the General Conference of the New Church (London), must have been very rapid, since in 1910 he responds to an invitation to the International Congress on Swedenborg celebrated in London. It is at this point that his work in spreading the life, ideas, and doctrines of Emanuel Swedenborg takes place.

The Swedenborgian public outreach that Andersen accomplished in Spain was channeled fundamentally through three events. The first is the founding of the Swedenborg Society of Spain (henceforth SSS), then the Spanish translation of some of the Swedish author's books, and, most importantly, his position as the sole publisher of the *Heraldo de la Nueva Iglesia* (henceforth HNC).

There exists no official document that makes reference to the founding of the SSS.[47] In one issue of HNC from 1934 there is a plea for the creation of such a society, but nevertheless, from the publication of the first HNC in 1915, it appears as an "organ of the SSS for the establishment and promotion of the New Church, that is, the true Christian religion in Spain." Thus, we may consider 1915 as the date the organization was founded, though in reality the existence of the SSS was purely in name only, since we believe that J. H. Andersen was the only member of that institution.[48] This is a reflection of the lack of resonance that it had, and it explains why news of Andersen and his activities appear nowhere. And of course, the SSS never resulted in any form of worship in the New Church, in spite of numbers 67 and 68 of the second volume of the HNC having "Instructions for the Faithful of the New Church" written by Andersen.[49]

The most tangible expression of the work of the SSS (that is, of Andersen) was the HNC, the "monthly religious newspaper neither Catholic nor Protestant." In fact, from 1915 until 1936 Andersen was editing almost continuously, driven by his neophyte zeal, what has been the most important specimen of Swedenborgism in the Spanish language (together with the work of the Mexican Dr. Calleja; see note 50 of this chapter). The HNC (also produced in Valencia, in the print shop of F. Vives Mora & Son, 8 Hernán Cortés Street), was organized by Andersen into four volumes: the first volume goes from 1915 to 1920 and occupies numbers 1 through 72; the second goes from 1921 to 1926 and also consists of numbers 1 through 72 (logically, the numbering of each newspaper begins anew with each volume); the third, 1927–1933, goes from 1 through 68 (this interruption is undoubtedly due to Andersen's economic problems in paying for the publication of the HNC), and the fourth, from 1934 to April 1936, consists of numbers 1 through 28. The civil war ended the HNC, the SSS, and all Andersen's public activity.

We can group the content of the HNC into three sections. The first consists of partial or complete translations of Swedenborg's books and booklets, translations done by Andersen himself from English versions, possibly contrasted with Swedish editions. This may be the most interesting aspect of the HNC, since they were the first translations of Swedenborg in Spanish on record.[50] The following works of the wise Swede were translated, partially or completely, in the pages of HNC: *La Verdadera Religión Cristiana* (*True Christianity,* extracts from volume 1); *El Cielo y sus maravillas, y el Infierno* (*Heaven and Hell,* idem extracts); *Memorabilia* (visionary narrations literarily distinct from the preceding texts begin to appear in the second volume of *Revelation Unveiled* beginning in 1766); *Las tierras en nuestro sistema solar y las tierras en el espacio sideral* (*Earths in Our Solar System and Earths in Outer Space*), which consisted of extracts from *De Telluribus* (*The Earths in Our Solar System,* also translated *The Worlds in Space* and *Other Planets*); *El Gran Hombre, que es el Cielo* (*The Great Man, That is Heaven*), extracted from *Secrets of Heaven,* idem; *Doctrina de la Caridad* (*The Doctrine of Charity*), extracted from *Secrets of Heaven* volume 3; *Doctrina Nueva Jerusalén sobre la Sagrada Escritura* (*Doctrine of Sacred Scripture*), idem; *Continuación de El Ultimo Juicio* (*Continuation on the Last Judgment,* also translated *Supplements*), p. 335 ff, idem; *Doctrina de la Nueva Jerusalén sobre la Fe* (*Doctrine of Faith*), p. 338 ff, idem; *La Nueva Jerusalén y su Celestial Doctrina* (*The New Jerusalem and its Heavenly Doctrine*), p. 12 ff, idem; *El Ultimo Juicio y Babilonia destruida* (*The Last Judgment and Babylon Destroyed*), p. 167 ff, idem; *Doctrina de la Vida para la Nueva Jerusalén* (*Doctrine of Life*), p. 166 ff, idem.

Besides all this, Andersen published some of the translations that appeared in the HNC in separate books. These were: *El Cielo y sus maravillas y el Infierno, de cosas oídas y vistas* (*Heaven and Its Wonders* and Hell, from *Things Heard and Seen*), Valencia, 1910 (this translation was revised by S. Alice Worcester and published under the auspices of the American Swedenborg Printing and Publishing Society of New York, which we assume collaborated financially on the publication); *La Nueva Jerusalén. Lo que es, lo que de ella dicen las Sagradas Escrituras y cómo se manifiesta en la tierra (The New Jerusalem: What It Is, What Scriptures Say about It, and How It Is Manifested on Earth)*, Valencia, 1910; *La Verdadera Religión Cristiana conteniendo la teología universal de la Nueva Iglesia (True Christian Religion, containing the Universal Theology of the New Church)*, Valencia, 1911 (this edition is cited by J. L. Borges; it is not complete); *Arcanos Celestes y Apocalipsis Revelado (Secrets of Heaven and Apocalypse Revealed)*, Valencia, 1914 (extracts; it was reissued by El Peregrino Publishers, Buenos Aires, 1984).

As can be shown, the translations of Swedenborg's works were published in book form before they appeared in the HNC, which makes us think that the SSS already existed, at least in the mind of J. H. Andersen (we have already said that the SSS was never officially registered). The translations tend to be correct, notwithstanding an occasional spelling or grammatical error. As we have stated, they are translated from English (possibly compared with Swedish editions), though we don't rule out the possibility that Andersen had the original Latin at hand, since he possessed a Latin dictionary (*Nuevo Diccionario latino-español*, by Raimundo de Miguel and Marqués de Morante, 12th edition, Madrid, 1903) and various books in that language.

Apart from the translations of Swedenborg, the pages of the HNC were filled with informational or devotional contributions from Andersen or well-known figures of the English or North American New Church,[51] biographical sketches of Swedenborg, allegorical and symbolic interpretations of books of the Bible, and articles referring to current events. Also included was a hymnal for prayers, with music by F. A. Reisiger. The contributions from New Church theologians (probably translations from Andersen himself), all Anglo-Saxons, include the following: William A. Presland, J. C. Ager, Edward Madeley, Chauncy Giles, E. C. Mitchel, W. L. Worcester, Frank Homes, Theodore Pitcairn, Julian K. Smyth, Foster W. Freeman, and many others. Among this jungle of Anglo names one Hispanic stands out, specifically, a Cuban: José de Armas.

José de Armas was born in Guanabacoa, Cuba, in 1866 and died in Havana on December 28, 1915. He wrote in Havana's *El Mundo* and was a correspondent in this city of the *New York Herald*. He lived in Madrid, where he worked as a correspondent of the Royal Academy of the Spanish Language and of the Hispanic-American Society. He left an ample bibliography: *El Quijote de Avellaneda y sus críticos (Don Quixote de Avellaneda and His Critics), La Dorotea de Lope (Dorotea of Lope), Cervantes y su época (Cervantes and His Times), Historia y literatura (History and Literature), Ensayo crítico sobre la literatura inglesa y española (Critical Essay on English and Spanish Literature), Cervantes en la literatura inglesa (Cervantes in English Literature), Cervantes y el Quijote (Cervantes and Don Quixote), Cervantes y el Duque de Sesa (Cervantes and the Duke of Sesa)*, and so on. He founded the magazine *Las Avispas* and wrote articles in *El Mundo* with information on the New Church. His contributions to the HNC were: "Un artículo sobre Swedenborg" ("An Article about Swedenborg"), vol. 1, p. 339; and "Una aplicación swedenborgiana" ("A Swedenborgian Study"), ibid., p. 365. His son Nicolás was also devoted to the New Church.

Generally speaking, the articles in the HNC are quite tedious, not moving beyond the moralizing applications of Swedenborgian doctrines. Of much more interest are the contributions of Andersen himself. Among the multitude of articles he wrote for the HNC, we will focus on "La divinidad de la Sagrada Escritura" ("The Divinity of Sacred Scripture"), vol. 2, no. 22–28. In reality, the article isn't signed, but the style is Andersen's; in it he posits with great clarity the limitations of a vulgarly literal biblical exegesis. Andersen contributes solutions that are accepted today by biblical science and proposes spiritual comprehension of the text through internalization. Another of Andersen's writings published in the HNC worth mentioning is "La Iglesia a través de los siglos" ("The Church through the Centuries"), vol. 1, p. 4–183, which had appeared earlier in the form of a booklet (Valencia, 1914). It is an abstract of Swedenborg's works, centered on an issue that seems to constantly concern Andersen: what we could call the ecclesiological aspect of Swedenborgianism.

Other noteworthy texts by Andersen include "Una breve biografía de Swedenborg" ("A Brief Biography of Swedenborg"), which is based on a work by Benjamin Worcester, *Swedenborg: Harbinger of the New*

Age of the Christian Church (Philadelphia: J. B. Lippincott Co., 1910). Andersen's biography, which appeared in volume 3, pages 41–93, is an excellent and well-informed summary. He also wrote a large quantity of articles based upon Swedenborgian ideas, such as "La segunda venida del Señor y la instauración de la Nueva Iglesia" ("The Second Coming of the Lord and the Instituting of the New Church"), "De Edén a Edén" ("From Eden to Eden"), and so on. Another important group of articles and editorials was motivated by current events, such as "La Nueva Iglesia y la ciencia" ("The New Church and Science"), where he expounds on the compatibility between Swedenborg's doctrines and the advances of science; "El fracaso del comunismo" ("The Failure of Communism"), which was very prophetic; "El ocaso del ultramontanismo, España, y el Vaticano. Se establecerá en concordato" ("The Decline of Ultramontanism, Spain, and the Vatican: An Agreement Will Be Reached"), where Andersen pleads for the freedom of worship. In this sense, in an editorial from January 1932 (volume 3), Andersen congratulates himself "for the new laws of the nation that allow us to announce with total freedom the truths of the New Church, without any risk of being bothered by the Roman Catholic hierarchy," and he laments in passing that the campaign for support of the SSS, which had been initiated with the previous issue of the HNC, hadn't been successful.

The tone of the HNC (in its pronouncements, its opinions, and its criticisms) is deliberate and well thought out. The criticisms that may appear are not reactionary, nor is there harshness in them, and they are always addressed to the Catholic hierarchy. In fact, in issue number 68 of volume 3, a call is made to the "lower clergy" to adopt an internalist attitude toward Christianity that is based on a spiritual interpretation of Scripture (for Andersen this means to accept the premises of the New Church). The vision that shines throughout all the issues of the HNC is the following: Swedenborg does more than just contribute new ideas or beliefs to Christianity; he proposes an inner experience and a deeper and more spiritual comprehension of Scripture. Thus the rationalizing nature of the articles we read in the HNC (in Andersen as well as in other authors). In fact, Swedenborg's ideas are considered above all as a rational and moral interpretation of the Christian faith, interpretation in perfect agreement with scientific discoveries of that era (many articles go in that direction). For the HNC, Swedenborg is an apostle of the agreement between reason and faith, of a purely spiritual worship, of progress, and of world peace.

World War I left its mark in the pages of HNC, as is shown in various article titles: "Después de la Guerra" ("After the War") by Andersen; "La reparación de la Guerra" ("War Reparations"), signed with the initials E. M. L. G.; and others in a similar vein. Swedenborg is also seen as a prophet of democracy and of social harmony, through titles such as "Verdadera democracia" ("True Democracy") by Andersen, "El mundo social" ("The Social World") by Andersen, etc. All of this attempts to portray Swedenborg as a discoverer of the true Christian message. This is far from the Romantic vision of the wise Swede. Certainly whoever reads the HNC could verify how far Andersen was from the occultist, theosophical, and Masonic currents so in fashion in that time period, currents that the uninformed may have connected with the name of Swedenborg.

The spirit that inspired Andersen, the HNC, and the SSS (in reality the same thing) was the furthest thing possible from a sect or esoteric sanctum, as is reflected in titles such as "La Nueva Iglesia no es una secta" ("The New Church Is Not a Sect") and "Algo sobre el espiritismo" ("Something about Spiritism"). Andersen's ideas could not have been more open or put forward with more clarity. They could not have been written in any other way, because for him Swedenborg came precisely to clarify the mysteries of Christianity and to show its compatibility with the discovered truths of reason and science. Andersen's idea of Christianity is based on an inner life where experiences of consciousness acquire more importance than formal, external rites. Therefore, according to what we can gather from Andersen's writings, to convert to the New Church does not involve any special act, nor does it mean joining a different institution, but rather it means to deepen the inner and spiritual experience of the meaning of Scripture, which results in a personalized Christianity free from any spurious elements (in this, Andersen's idea of Swedenborg seems quite fitting).

Finally, we need to consider the repercussions of the SSS and the HNC. In this regard, we can say that J. H. Andersen's enthusiasm was a complete failure (we have already mentioned how he recognized that in one of his editorials). In number 68 of volume 3 (1934), he affirms that "few are those who have shown appreciation toward the teachings of the New Church." On the other hand, we know that the HNC was received in Puerto Rico, Argentina, Brazil, the Philippines, and Cuba, but there are no lists available of possible subscribers, which may have been able to contribute relevant data. At any rate, Andersen's initiatives vanished like a shadow. Proof of this lies in the enormous difficulty in finding any issues of the HNC, and in the absence of citations in other authors, press, or magazines of the era.[52] Sociologically speaking, the role that Swedenborg could have played in Spain was held by theosophy or Masonry: Mario Roso de Luna or Arturo Soria would have been excellent Swedenborgians.

Andersen's efforts were as generous and enthusiastic as they were ineffectual. But at any rate, we are left with his translations of Swedenborg and his refined intuitions, which merit a place in the history of religious ideas of contemporary Spain.

9

RELATIONSHIPS AND INFLUENCES

Swedenborg and Kierkegaard

Swedenborg's relationship to existentialism, and to Søren Kierkegaard in particular, has already been expressed elsewhere. Authors such as Bergquist, Milosz, Boyer, and myself have spoken of the existential character of Swedenborg's doctrine, and in this sense it has been compared to Pascal, Kierkegaard, Dostoevski, or Unamuno. What is it that justifies labeling Swedenborg as an existentialist? We see a general consensus that understands existentialism as any doctrine or philosophy that requires not just an intellectual acceptance, but also, and above all, an inner and personal experience. It is evident that this definition (which is certainly applicable to Swedenborg) is too broad, but if we more concretely contrast Swedenborg's ideas with those of other authors, we will see how they often coincide with his existential proposals.

This is reflected exceptionally well in one of Swedenborg's works. We are referring to the *Journal of Dreams*, a text that collects his mystical experiences and, we shall soon see, demonstrates an existential philosophy toward mystical phenomena.

In the *Journal of Dreams* we find a full array of terms that denote this special quality of what is lived intimately and personally. For example: *nåd* (grace), *förstand* (intelligence), *helge ande* (Holy Spirit), *kärleken* (love), *frestelsen* (temptation), *synd* (sin), *ovärdilighet* (indignity), *innerliga glädie* (inner happiness), *ängslan* (desperation), *fruchtan och bäfwan* (fear and trembling), *förtviflan* (desperation), *retta tror* (righteous faith), *förtröstar* (confidence), *inwertes principien* (internal principle), *inwertes meniskian* (internal human), *utwertes meniskian* (external human), *sig på nåd och onåd* (freeing oneself), etc. All these expressions, in the context of the strong, decisive spiritual crisis from which they arise, take on the existential stamp to which we refer, in this case inseparable from a mystical life experience. We will choose a few examples that reflect the existential struggle and agony of the *Journal of Dreams*:

> Afterwards I went out and saw many black images; one was thrown to me. I saw that it had no use of its foot. This meant, I think, that natural reason could not accommodate to spiritual reason. . . . It was strange that I was able to have two thoughts at one and the same time and quite distinct from one another . . . Yes, I have also observed that our whole will, which we have inherited and which is ruled by the body and introduces thoughts into the mind, is opposed to the spirit. For this reason, there is continual strife . . . I was continually in combat against these double thoughts *(dubbla tanckar)* that battled against each other . . . I was all day in equivocal thoughts, which tried to destroy the spiritual . . . I was this day by turns in interior anxiety *(inwertes änglan)* and sometimes in despair *(förtwiflan)* . . . For a number of days in succession, I was usually for some hours in a state of spiritual anxiety *(andelig ängslan)*, without being able to tell the cause, although I seemed to be assured of the grace of God. . . . It was an anguish in the soul, but not in the senses, without any pain at all in the body.[1]

The existential character of Swedenborg's thought can also be compared with that of Blaise Pascal. Indeed, there are profound equivalencies between the two thinkers. We cannot analyze all of these similarities in our limited study, but we will point out some of them. First of all, we need to note that the mysticism of both thinkers is Christ-centric, rather than a speculative mysticism of the Neoplatonic type. In fact, the two authors start from a certain questioning of their scientific or philosophical thought. Let us think about this statement from Pascal: "God of Abraham, God of Isaac, God of Jacob, not of the philosophers, nor of the wise men" and compare it with this phrase taken from the *Journal of Dreams:* "To the highest be praise, honor, and glory! Hallowed be his name! Holy, holy, Lord God Zabaoth!"[2] or with this one: "I believed and I didn't believe, and I thought that because of this the angels and God show themselves to shepherds and not to the philosopher who intervenes with his understanding." Pascal's distinction between the spirit of finesse and the spirit of geometry has its counterpart in the Swede through differences such as internal and external human, natural and spiritual reason, etc. Likewise, for both, reflections on the mathematical point acquire a special importance as boosters and drivers of their philosophical and theological constructions. Ultimately, Pascal and Swedenborg should be seen as a reaction against rationalism from within rationalism itself.

The relationship of Emanuel Swedenborg with Søren Kierkegaard is described in a very indirect way by Eric Peterson in an article titled "Kierkegaard and Protestantism." In this article Peterson presents the Dane and the Swede as two critics of Protestantism in general and of Scandinavian Protestantism in particular. More precisely, according to Peterson, both would attack—each one in his own way—nominalism, the idea of *sola fide* (justification by faith alone), and forensic justification, that is, the fundamental assumptions of the Protestant Reformation and the consequences that it entailed: leaving the human soul in loneliness and inner isolation. As stated earlier, Peterson's idea about Swedenborg and Kierkegaard is enormously suggestive, and it certainly enables one to approach the existential elements they share. We should, then, without forcing the texts, attempt to establish the possible affiliation that would unite Swedenborg with Kierkegaard.

Eric Peterson's proposal seems to us not only interesting but also completely justified. In fact, a common theme in Swedenborg and Kierkegaard is the rejection of *sola fide* and forensic justification and the affirmation of free will, with all the corollaries that this carries. According to Peterson, Kierkegaard and Swedenborg react against the solipsistic lack of communication in which Lutheranism encloses the human soul by means of justification by faith alone, without any recourse to works, that is, to liberty. It is true that for Swedenborg this is a crucial topic, and so the doctrine of the communion of the saints acquires a great importance in his system. This is an issue that for him becomes angelology and, as a totalizing category, takes the name of the *homo maximus*, communicating the perfect organic relationship of all the members that make up the spiritual community of saints or angels. For the Swede the figure of the angel (or of the saint, since for him they coincide) represents continual spiritual opening and thus the possibility of completely fulfilling its internal dynamic. It is in a strict sense an existence, a being that comes out of itself, that is pure internal communication with no need for external mediation. In other words, angelology, as an image of the communion of the saints, signifies the pure spontaneity of consciousness, spiritual fullness of the human being. On the contrary, according to Swedenborg, the punishment of the condemned consists of their radical isolation—what characterizes bad people is that they are closed and refuse to open themselves to the fulfillment of their potentialities (love and wisdom). We should interpret the figure of the *homo maximus* or angelic society in Swedenborg as a reclamation of the doctrine of the communion of saints, absent or with scarce presence in the Lutheran theology, depending on leaving the closed circle of *sola fide* and of the expansion of the spirit. In this way we understand the importance that Saint Paul has for Swedenborg, since Pauline theology serves the mystic Swede not only as an affirmation of the primacy of works, but also for sustaining the doctrine of the mystical body of Christ, that is, the communion of saints and the spiritual church. In addition, Swedenborg had a precedent very close to the postulation of the communion of saints: his own father, the bishop and theologian Jesper Svedberg, had written about it in his *Catechismi gudeliga öfning* (Skara, 1709). As we shall see, Swedenborg's religiosity has its antecedents in Nordic pietism.

Swedenborg's defense of free will and the importance of works for salvation is well known. In fact, to a great extent all his writing flows in this direction and contrarily serves as a rejection of predestination and justification by faith alone. A consequence of this is the privileged position that love, kindness, volition, and affections (versus intellectual faculties) possess as the authentic driving forces behind Swedenborg's life and thought. The defense of free will and of the value of works becomes an obsession for Swedenborg. To this is added a harsh criticism of *servo arbitrio* (bound choice) and *sola fide,* as he shows in a representative manner when he describes the circumstances under which Luther, Calvin, and Melanchthon meet in the afterlife (it is the worst stop).

The openness and communication where the essence of the human soul resides, according to Swedenborg, is reflected in the importance that the term *societas* has for him. It is a term that is at the same time collective and individual, since the reality that it represents is fulfilled not quantitatively, but rather qualitatively. Swedenborg's *societas* is one and all, since it depends not on the amount but rather on the intensity of love, goodness, and truth (which abound in their open state). A similar process occurs with *ecclesia,* another fundamental word for Swedenborg (as we saw in chapter 5), which also should be seen as an ontological determination that above all depends on the intensity and depth with which spiritual realities can be lived.

The *societas* in its fullness is, then, the communion of saints or angels, a category fundamental to Swedenborg's entire system. Angelology in Swedenborg signifies the opening of the soul to other souls, to other densities of being, of love, and of intelligence. It also signifies the presence of the spiritual and divine in a world—in contrast to a Pascal whose thought was close to Jansenism—that had cloistered itself in mundane reality, blurring the signs of God's manifestation. For Swedenborg that presence continues to have meaning: there is no gap between heaven and earth because there is an *influxus* that connects the two spheres. Here we see that Swedenborg's attitude is totally different from Pascal's, no matter how much they coincide on other issues.

As can be shown, we find ourselves with elements that make applying the term existentialist to Swedenborg something more than a mere analogy: we should understand his existentialism in the sense of human opening and of being open.

We stated earlier that an attempt to search for a comparison between Kierkegaard and Swedenborg does not require any forcing of texts. It is evident that there are differences between the two authors, as is normal for two thinkers with more than a century's worth of distance between them. Swedenborg is on balance a child of the Enlightenment and of Cartesianism, and science occupies a central position within his philosophical-religious problems, precisely because it is about adapting reason and faith (together with other motifs central to Protestantism). For Kierkegaard the essential issue lies in clarifying the role of Christianity in light of Hegel and Schleiermacher (and also, as Peterson affirms, in light of Lutheranism). Though the circumstances are different, undoubtedly there are significant analogies in the positions of the Swede and the Dane with respect to the metaphysical and theological statutes of Christianity. We will proceed, then, using as a common thread an analysis of their confrontation with the doctrine of justification by faith.

Certainly one could approach other motifs of the two authors, for example, the influence of pietism in their religiosity. We know that Swedenborg had a close relationship with pietistic circles and also that he was influenced by figures such as Arnold, Dippel, and Zinzendorf. However, these relationships are not decisive, since we know that later Swedenborg distanced himself from the Herrnhutians (the pietistic current with the most ascendancy in Scandinavia). Also, in Swedenborg's posthumously published book *Spiritual Experiences* he harshly criticized Zinzendorf (precisely because of the attitude of passive piety that Zinzendorf preached), and in the same volume we see that criticism reflected in a representative form in the visions Swedenborg records. In any case, we need to keep in mind that pietism also entailed a reaction against official Protestantism in that it restored a perceptible and emotional piety, and thus logically it is a basic element of both Swedenborg's and Kierkegaard's theologies.

However, when we give Kierkegaard as an example of the reaction against the entrapment of humans in Lutheran fideism, we are presented with the common view of Kierkegaardian thought as a powerful, metaphysical individualism, where affirmations of the One appear as the most decisive instantiations of his religious philosophy. In this respect Henry Corbin (certainly a great Swedenborgian and Kierkegaardian) in his article "L'humour dans son rapport avec l'historique chez Hamann et chez Kierkegaard" ("The History of Humor in Relation to Hamann and Kierkegaard"), points out that the idea of the isolated human being is essential in Protestant Christianity, and he cites the Dane speaking of "the isolation of the individual conditioned by the Reform." In another place Kierkegaard affirms this himself when he states that "society is a determination inferior to the individual" (*Practice in Christianity*). Naturally, we will not analyze all the citations that could be brought to light. Without a doubt there is a dimension in Kierkegaard in which his metaphysics of individual subjectivity is clearly affirmed.

What can we say about the thought-provoking proposal of a Kierkegaard who is critical of Lutheran solipsism and of Protestantism in general? First of all, they are not incompatible, and of course the ontology of the One can be reconciled with a critical attitude. In addition, it is often overlooked that there is another Kierkegaard, apart from the one who is most known and cited regarding anguish, sin, fear, and trembling. There is the Kierkegaard of *Works of Love*. Is not Kierkegaard the philosopher of solitary individualism? We need to know more about the other Kierkegaard, the one of *Works of Love*, which is certainly his most voluminous work, and above all his *The Lily of the Field, the Bird of the Air* (as the title suggests, this book is a commentary on Matthew 6:26–30). On another occasion we have stated that Kierkegaard is not only a great philosopher and theologian, but also a great exegete. The image of the Dane that we have here completely balances the other, a bit somber, which we usually have of him.

It is very significant that Kierkegaard as well as Swedenborg insist on love as a concomitant impulse to free will, since it is works of love that remove us from the isolation in which *sola fide* had imprisoned the human being. Works of love signify opening and communication. Kierkegaard truly has a consistent dimension in the absolute foundation of the I, that is, of the individualized individual *(enkelte)*. But this absolute foundation of subjectivity can come only from an Absolute Thou, and from this perspective one can understand the collection of philosophical and theological categories characterized as belonging to Kierkegaard. Only when an ontologically based consciousness is not dissipated in pure external sensibility can one begin to yield to works of love. This second Kierkegaard, the one of the works of love, resembles Saint Francis of Assisi, a wise Taoist, or a Zen Buddhist more than the customary image of the dour theologian. Instead, we see a shining disengagement and spontaneity of the spirit. Clearly this condition brought about by works of love (one that we cannot hesitate to call mystical) could be construed as a theory about communication among subjectivities, that is, a pneumatological ecclesiology. Yet we believe this issue is better resolved in Swedenborg, since angelology smooths out the problem of communication of consciousnesses, in that the angel signifies the open transparency of the soul.

Undoubtedly Peterson's intriguing proposals have many more nuances to explore and develop. For example, another element that connects Swedenborg to Kierkegaard is their personalism, since individual and personal determination has the same metaphysical weight for the Swedish visionary as for the Dane. In any case, we believe the comparison between Kierkegaard and Swedenborg is more than justified in relation to a Scandinavian reformist criticism and, more specifically, a criticism of nominalism and of the doctrine of justification by faith alone. The Kierkegaardian *aut–aut* (either–or) also applies to Swedenborg, given the Swede's assertion that a fundamental aspect of human life consists of choosing between good and evil. Both thinkers are connected by a deeply felt recognition of free will, an original and pristine freedom of choice with fear, agony, and ecstasy.

Swedenborg and Henry Corbin

The habitual reader of Corbin will have confirmed that the figure of Emanuel Swedenborg appears with notorious frequency in the works of the French philosopher and Islamologist. This citational recurrence is not, of course, mere coincidence. On the contrary, it reveals the mystical Swede's clear and profound influence on Corbin's works. In fact, Corbin continually mentions Swedenborg in comparison to a varied litany of Islamic philosophers and mystics—above all, Shiites. For example, Avicenna, Ibn 'Arabi, Sohravardi, Ruzbihan Baqli Sirazi, and many others are placed in relation to the ideas and experiences of the Swedish visionary. In this sense Corbin introduces an essential methodology for the comparative study of Western and Eastern spiritualities.

Given this frequent presence, a knowledge of Swedenborg is fundamental to truly understanding Corbin's thought. Inversely, the understanding that Corbin has of Swedenborg can help us penetrate Swedenborg's ideas. In fact, Corbin has provided us with an extraordinarily lucid interpretation of Swedenborg's essential message, dispensing with the more or less anecdotal details that always accompany the figure of Swedenborg and that at times distort his message. Let us proceed, then, in investigating the issue.

Naturally, the abundant references to Swedenborg in the Corbin's texts immediately show us the substantial influence of the Nordic on Corbin. In fact, we believe that together with Louis Massignon, Etienne Gilson, Cassirer, Heidegger, and a few others, Swedenborg is part of the foundation (by way of stimulus and inspiration) of the immense investigation that Corbin conducted into the spiritual world, both Western and Eastern.

We will attempt to synthesize the motifs that in our judgment explain the influence of Emanuel Swedenborg on Henry Corbin. In the first place, we believe that we should mention Corbin's inclination toward a reformist Christianity of a type that is more spiritual than institutional. Thus his preference for figures such as Schwenckfeld, Frank, Boehme, and of course Swedenborg himself. These are figures who conceive of Christianity as an inner, spiritual experience, where the legal aspects stay subordinated to the individual and internal experiences (this is the meaning that Corbin attributes to the esoteric, versus the exoteric or external). In this sense Swedenborg represents a decisive influence, since Corbin always showed himself to be an essentially Christian thinker, and his religiosity conditioned his university research. In some ways the influence on Corbin of the other determinations of Swedenborg's categories depend on the fact of Corbin's Christianity, which is demonstrated in the priority given to the symbolic over the historical. We shall now look at some of the motivations that explain Corbin's interest in the mystic of the North.

One motivation that seems fundamental is hermeneutics. It is not a coincidence that this is the subject of the only systematic work that Corbin devotes to comparing Swedenborg and Shiite thought: "Herméneutique spirituelle comparée (I. Swedenborg –II. Gnose ismaélienne)" ("Comparison of Spiritual Hermeneutics [I. Swedenborg—II. Ismailian Gnosis]," 1964). The title is in itself quite expressive: what Corbin finds in Swedenborg that is transferable to the experience of comprehension for the Shiite is the type of spiritual interpretation that the Swede carries out on the biblical text. What connects Swedenborg's exegesis with that of the Shiite is the shared method of interpreting sacred text (be it the Bible or the Koran) as a "narrative of the soul": a description of events that happen in the inner world of each one of the interpreters, who make the message their own. In short, it is the spiritual interpretation as opposed to the historicist that likens Swedenborg to the Shiite. Corbin will especially focus on this aspect, given his hermeneutical and phenomenological interests.

Rather than a literal, formal, or legal exegesis, Corbin offers an understanding of the text as a symbol that reveals its meaning in the consciousness of and for the person who is interpreting. The long and dense article to which we alluded is a model treatise of comparative phenomenology and hermeneutics. This spiritual and personal aspect of hermeneutics ties in with the Christian vision of which we spoke earlier: to live out biblical narratives as "events of the soul" means affirming the personal determination of the spirit. It is important to consider the hermeneutical issue as a factor that explains Corbin's interest in Swedenborg, given that the interpretive and phenomenological relationship—from a vital and individual point of view with respect to the Book—was a constant and guiding force for all Corbin's activities.

Undoubtedly there may be many motifs that justify a comparison between Swedenborg and Shiism or Sufism. Of course, these motifs abound thanks to the constant influence of the visionary Swede on Corbin. However, we will examine only one argument that seems to us decisive, if we keep in mind where the center of interest in Corbin's philosophy lies. We allude to Swedenborg's representative and figurative metaphysics. In fact, in the visionary experiences that the Nordic transmits to us in his works, we find a constant transformation of philosophical concepts and categories into images and representations, so that throughout Swedenborg's spiritual narratives we observe the constitution of and authentic metaphysics of the figure, the icon, the determination.

In fact, in Swedenborg everything abstract tends to convert to concrete and personal determination, to form itself, according to the dilations and expansions of the consciousness. We are very far from a mysticism of the ineffable where the individual is dissolved in the bosom of an undifferentiated Absolute. Thus angelology is of crucial importance in Swedenborg (Eugeni d'Ors envisioned this very clearly), and of course it forms part of Corbin's overriding interest in Swedenborg. Certainly the image of the angel summarizes quite well what we referred to earlier about the metaphysics of representation: the angel translates an idea into images, making it comprehensible. That is to say, the angel is the hermeneutic of the higher concept, living it not as an intelligible connection but rather as a personal experience.

Clearly this dimension of Swedenborg's transcendental experiences is favorable for comparison to this ample sphere of Islamic spirituality, in its Sufi, Ismailian, or Sohravardian variants. Corbin studied this meticulously, and it can be summarized under the terms of *mundus imaginalis, 'alam al-mizal,* or *Malakut:* a world of images where "the spirits make bodies and spiritualize them." That is, they make a segment of the mediation between the intelligible and the material. The ontological limit *(bárzaj)* that belongs to the realm of metaphysical and spiritual categories manifests its contents in a figurative and representative way, to thus configure them and make them accessible to human experience. This same experience is shaped by that world of images, which appears as the personal contents of the same consciousness (the angel of *each* person). Here, in the *mundus imaginalis* as in the Swedenborgian heaven, we observe a phenomenology of image-based consciousness that delineates an ontological realm in which time and space become internal places and a fluidity of the soul, and in which locations and events express the plasticity of the life of the spirit. The works of Swedenborg (like the visions of Avicenna, Sohravardi, and Ibn 'Arabi, and like what is described in many other documents of Ismailian philosophy) show us a sphere of reality that is not the sphere of the purely intelligible nor of decadent sensibility, nor of arbitrary fable, nor of linear history; this sphere is the ontological reality of the symbol, of the mediation, of the figurative representation (thus its literary expression is made through narratives, which are nothing more than narratives of what occurs in the soul).

In this vision of image-based worlds we perceive footprints of platonic ideas, of the soul of the world of *Timaeus,* of the Abrahamic and Zoroastrian angelologies (Daena, Holy Spirit, Angel Gabriel), and of the agent Understanding. Henry Corbin understood how to unite Swedenborg's experience with the mystical experience of Sufism and of the Shiite through the idea of symbol as a living reality that demands a continuous, effective actualization (here hermeneutics, ontology, and spirituality converge). Henry Corbin has managed to enlighten us with a more profound understanding of Swedenborg and of the immense wealth of oriental Islamic philosophy. All this certainly expands our understanding of Corbin's own thought: the light that he contributes toward the understanding of Swedenborg is what serves us also in our understanding of his vital and intellectual trajectory.

In conclusion, in reading Corbin we envision an existential and personalist Swedenborg, a Swedenborg who reveals a phenomenology of the symbol and of consciousness.

Ibn 'Arabi and Swedenborg: Proposals for a Figurative Philosophy

Before we proceed, we will demarcate the notion of figurative philosophy with which we will operate here. Examining the roots, we see that the problem lies in the relationship between representation and concept. Reality can be expressed and captured through a conceptual and intelligible discourse (the Logos), and through a representative discourse whose determinations are narrative, image, and figure (myth). Naturally, these discourses are not exclusive, and the history of ideas continually shows us how in the same author Logos (concept) and myth (narrative) can exist side by side: Parmenides, Plato, Avicenna, or Sohravardi are some examples, but of course not the only ones. Clearly, figurative thought is, in essence, representation.

Therefore, a philosophy of the figure will transform these concepts into images and will convert the metaphysical relationships (intelligible and unitary) into consecutive narratives (thus plural). But it is not only concepts or philosophical categories that are susceptible to being expressed in representative discourse. All profound or transcendental experiences will tend to arrange themselves in narrative form. One might say that they need to be converted into narrative in order to acquire essential form. An outstanding example of this is mysticism. In fact, mysticism as an experience of the ineffable requires a symbol that embodies what is ineffable in the experience itself. Symbol, metaphor, or parable become the privileged language of narrative, since they form in a tangible way what could not be expressed in any other manner. Consequently, a philosophy of the figure deviates from what is conceptual, yet without opposing it. A philosophy of the figure also avoids what is ineffable or indeterminate, since it works toward determining in images and representations that which otherwise would remain inaccessible. Emanuel Swedenborg and Muhyiddin Ibn 'Arabi are two excellent examples of this figurative thought.

Emanuel Swedenborg, as discussed elsewhere in this volume, was a scientist, philosopher, theologian, and visionary whose vast work (close to three hundred titles, counting booklets and manuscripts) responds to the typical problems of the eighteenth century, that is, those that involve Cartesianism, deism, the Enlightenment, or mechanism. Dichotomies such as God/world, spirit/matter, or soul/body are of special concern to Swedenborg (the soul/body dichotomy occupies a large part of his philosophical work). The Swede's intellectual agenda is to resolve these dualities. Along with this we also find purely theological issues arising from Lutheranism, such as the polarities of faith/reason or determinism/free will, which held great interest for Swedenborg. To this collection of issues we must add underlying problems related to the Bible and its exegesis. In this area the Nordic author proposes another dichotomy, this time between the superficial or literal meaning and the deep or spiritual meaning.

In short, Swedenborg is a thinker influenced by Aristotle, Descartes, Malebranche, Leibniz, and Wolff. Nevertheless, he has produced hardly any purely conceptual philosophical works.[3] The vast majority of the books from his philosophical-theological stage respond to a distinct form of expression, undoubtedly because they are due to a non-conceptual form of experience. This other form is representative, since in Swedenborg all concepts or categories tend to represent themselves, to convert themselves into figurative determination. The flows and expansions of the spirit substitute for ontological movements, by means of which Swedenborg's doctrine will be articulated through personal ideas. This is closely related to the positing of a figurative philosophy, since there is nothing more concrete and determined than the notion of person. This gives the doctrine an existential footprint, which has attracted the interest of authors such as Dostoevsky, Strindberg, Unamuno, or Corbin himself.

Three major threads run through the work of the Prophet of the North: a philosophy of the person in relation to transcendental reality, which lends a strongly existential—even existentialist or personalist—tenor to Swedenborg's system; a philosophy that is resolved in representations or images instead of pure concepts, which means that the symbolic worlds have priority over any other instantiation; a philosophy that is presented as inextricably linked to spirituality, thus a line of thought in which mystical life experience and conceptual speculation are reconciled and complementary: a philosophical knowledge, not merely accumulative, but essentially transformative. In summary, three ideas define the Swedish prophet: person, figure, and spiritual experience. The tendency to convert concept into narrative is evidenced in Swedenborg's use of the narratives called *memorabilia,* which appear starting in 1766 and that seem to be authentic narrative developments of philosophical-religious doctrines; we could rightly affirm that Swedenborg's theology merits the title of narrative theology.

A literary analysis of Swedenborg's works is fundamental for understanding the transformation of his thought, since that thought becomes embodied in writings with the same tenor as the content he wishes to express. For this reason, for each spiritual metamorphosis we find a distinct literary vehicle: *Worship and Love of God, Journal of Dreams, Spiritual Experiences, Secrets of Heaven,* etc., are narratives that stake out the internal evolution of the author.

Swedenborg is a visionary to whom the category of *mundus imaginalis*—the intermediate world between the purely intelligible and the perceptible or ontological sphere of the transcendental imagination, where pure ideas are first given form—fits well.[4] Therefore, following the trail blazed by Henry Corbin, we can integrate the Scandinavian mystic into a line of thought characterized by embodying the conceptual sphere in images and figures. It is not a mere transposition of philosophical categories with representations. It is about these same categories being experienced as representations and visualizations. By virtue of these characteristics (vital as well as intellectual) we can establish a spiritual affiliation where we may place Ibn 'Arabi and Swedenborg, among many others.

For this brief introduction to Ibn 'Arabi as mystic and figurative thinker, we will begin by referring to the Akbarian distinction between *tanzih* and *tashbih*. We understand *tanzih* as a negative or apophatic theology, the ineffable dimension of Absolute Unity (*via remotionis,* as Massignon translated the term), the highest transcendence. We understand *tashbih* (immanence) as cataphatic theology, that is, the dimension in which the contents of the One are manifested and determined. The *tanzih* speaks to us of the phase of divinity understood as absolute identity, and the *tashbih* of the plural articulation of this same identity. Clearly our discourse on Ibn 'Arabi as a figurative thinker belongs to the sphere of *tashbih,* that is, to the interpretation of reality as a plural manifestation of the determinations of the One. This means that our perspective of the mystic from Murcia is, consequently, as a thinker of Being as plurality and as a mystic of personal determination. It is within this context that we inscribe figurative philosophy. Let us now briefly examine how these characteristics are ordered.

If we had to summarize in some way the immense work of Ibn 'Arabi we would say that it responds to the following assumptions: starting with the idea of One, absolutely transcendent, and then submitting to a mode of being colored by an existential individualism and by an ontology of representation (we perceive the similarity with Swedenborg here). In this sense, a fundamental category of the Akbarian work lies in the notion of *tayalli,* that is, the universal manifestation of the One as theophany, which makes reality as a whole into a system of symbols and determinations of the One—and, as a consequence, determinations and substantive entities. We might also say figures, especially personal figures. We will now proceed to look at some of the more important figurative determinations.

Of course, the category that in my judgment responds most intensely to these ideas is the Divine Name. In the set of metaphysical determinations that is the *ad extra* revelation of divinity, the attributes and the names of God acquire a special importance, since they represent the ontological modes of what is beyond Being. But the idea of the Name in some ways stands out from any other consideration. This is because the Name is not just the externalization of an attribute, nor is it a metaphorical way of speaking of a divine function (here one can glimpse the influence of Asarí realism on Ibn 'Arabi). The Name is the effective and substantial pronouncement of a reality intrinsic to God himself. The articulation of the Name signifies a privileged way in which the determinations of the One occur. In other words, the theophanic process of revelation *(tayalli)* takes place through the Names. By means of the ninety-nine Names, divinity becomes symbolically present. No one can miss the similarity of the symbolic theology of Ibn 'Arabi here with that of Pseudo-Dionysus.

However, the Akbarian doctrine of the Names has another essential repercussion. The naming of each Name is not an abstract event, nor merely a relationship belonging to the categorical sphere. The naming of each Name is a statement that is personal to each one of us, and in this same statement we constitute ourselves personally and substantively. The divine names are pronounced for us. As Corbin would say, following Luther, we are the *significatio passiva* of each Name, the active part of the pronunciation corresponding to God. For example: if God is just, we are justified; if God is One, we are unified; if God is benevolent, we are made better.[5] Thus a reciprocal relationship is established between the signifier (God, who pronounces each Name) and the signified (each one of us that is named by each Name). In short, the Names are configurative determinations of our own personal reality, since in itself each name or word always designates a formal and determined entity (much more the divine word: Logos, *dabar*, or *calam*). The Names form part of the plural order of Being.

The doctrine of Names has more crucial consequences from a philosophical and spiritual point of view. First of all, it seems clear from this perspective that Akbarian mysticism leads to experiences of determination of consciousness and not of its dissolution in the bosom of an unfathomable abyss. The Name determines for us how we are essentially, and also personally; this is another key consequence that contributes to the figurative character of Ibn 'Arabi's system. In fact, as we stated earlier, the Divine Names are not only metaphysical attributes or modes, but rather personal labels that reveal people, and as such they are labels that show an identity itself, that is, a supreme identity. An identity for each Name is stated precisely to identify the person for whom it is said: the personal Name thus personalizes (we will see that this relationship has various modulations).[6] An objection could emerge in this vision we are presenting. Ibn 'Arabi's mysticism includes the idea of *fana'*, or dissolution of individuality as the final ecstasy of the mystical process. This conflicts with our personalistic perception of Ibn 'Arabi. It is also certain that together with *fana'* we find the term *baqa'*, meaning the continued existence of consciousness as an acquisition after the realization of the supreme experience. We can understand this duplicity as a consequence of the same bi-unity of the pronouncement of the Name, or alternatively as the acquisition of a persistent existence after the elimination of a spurious ego. Following Corbin, we find we need to speak of the personalistic mysticism of Ibn 'Arabi. Besides, as we stated earlier, different modulations of the theory of Names provide the personal and personalizing character of Akbarian spirituality. Thus, the relationship between lord and servant (an exact likeness of the relationship between lover and loved) also marks the form, in dependence itself, of the personal determination as essential determination.

Another derivation that is most important and of the most consequence to the doctrine of the Divine Names in Ibn 'Arabi stems from its hermeneutic implications. We have stated that each Name is not only the explanation of an attribute or ontological mode, but at the same time it is that content acting in each person who assumes it, who takes possession of it and internalizes it, that is, who interprets it. Each Name requires, then, an appropriation for each one of us, and that appropriation shapes us in our own determination. The appropriation requires a dependence on the meaning of the Name, and therefore a personal adoption, taking as our own what is stated in the Name. The adoption or appropriation of the Name *(tayalluq)*, which is what we are considering here as the interpretive movement itself, is one of the three actions that makes the Name's very being function: the other two are dependence *(ta'alluq)* or our need of the attributions of the Name in question; and the effective realization *(tahaqquq)* of the essence of the Name. As can be shown, it is a matter of these three forms harmonizing or articulating the act of assuming the meaning named for us.[7]

Swedenborg and Ibn 'Arabi are two authors whose thoughts and vital experiences are essentially conditioned by exegesis of the revealed Book. Here, of course, Ibn 'Arabi occupies a privileged position, given that all his spiritual experience is based on the interpretation of the Koran. In hermeneutics we find another point of connection with Swedenborg, for whom all theoretical systematization is derived from his inner, lived experience of the biblical content, which occurs not only in his theological era but even during the scientific period.[8] Thus, on occasion we have labeled the entirety of Swedenborg's work as midrashic, given that there is no end of exegetical referents. This also demonstrates that both the man from Murcia and the Swede navigate within the sphere of determination, as is expected from their hermeneutic activity. This consists essentially of explaining, developing, and bringing to light the scriptural content they gleaned. The same mystical character in Swedenborg and Ibn 'Arabi contributes to the development of hermeneutics through the spiritual experience of the Book. That is, the spiritual experience of the Book is the same as understanding its contents. The lived mystical experience, in this context of the philosophy of determination, achieves the fusion of horizons, opens up hidden meanings, and thus consolidates the very subjectivity of the subject. We believe that biblical and Koranic exegeses in general result in the constitution of hermeneutics. In other words, through the vital necessity of understanding the sacred Book, hermeneutical interpretation arises as an autonomous discipline. The revealed Book, rather than being an obstacle to the involvement of thought, presents itself to us as something that sparks the initiative to speculate and penetrate meaning.[9]

There is another decisive element in this order of things. I refer to the type of spirituality that animates and motivates the Akbarian's work: the importance that affective and voluntary factors acquire, both in the process of manifestation on the part of Divinity and on the part of the believers themselves in their relationship to Divinity. The creative impulse that produces the set of theophanies resulting from *absconditum* is mercy. In fact, for Ibn 'Arabi the Supreme Name is Rahmán, the Merciful, and his mercy is what moves the Absolute itself and its process of externalization. Likewise in Swedenborg, the principles of love and affection prevail over any others—not in vain are their roots found in pietism. We can also find great similarities with Kierkegaard, for whom, in spite of the elevated conceptualization of his thought, mercy and love are key categories.

As can be seen, all these characteristics affect the existential property of Ibn 'Arabi's spirituality: individual determination, personalism, precedence of volition, hermeneutics as concrete appropriation, and so on. All strive toward the figurative consideration of thought and of the same mystical experience.

In this brief and succinct exposition of the motifs that form a philosophy of the figure in the mystic from Murcia, one must include the notion of transcendental imagination *(jayal)*. The whole process of immanence stemming from the Supreme Unity, that is, the entire theophanic system, is conceived as a production of images that schematize pure ideas. In this way the totality of reality is presented as a kaleidoscope in which each image signifies a determined way of combining and pluralizing the Supreme Unity. This imagination in turn is divided in two: on the one hand, we have the transcendental imagination with its function of ontological schematization; on the other hand we have the human imagination in its receptive function of these same schematizations. We also have a realization of the reciprocal function created by both the projected image and the mirror that captures and reflects the image. This relationship constitutes the *mundus imaginalis* or *'alam al-mizal,* which is the sphere in which the subject finds its specific place (a place of forms, figures, and images); a place that accounts for not only the conceptual discourse, but more importantly the visionary account or the narrative of the experiences of the soul. This relates to what we stated earlier concerning the tendency to describe philosophical or theological differences and discussions in a personal and existential manner. For example, we have the discussions of Ibn 'Arabi with Mansur al-Hallaj, Bayazid Bastami, and other Sufi mystics. Likewise, Swedenborg describes conversations with Luther, Calvin, and Melanchthon; Sohravardi converses with Aristotle; and Ruzbihan Baqli of Shiraz in his visions has dialogs with other notable figures of Islamic mysticism. This is a clear example of how a conceptual conflict is accommodated through figurative delimitations.

The theme of transcendental imagination leads to the problem of passive versus active intellect. While in the earlier discussions the emphasis fell on the intellect, in Ibn 'Arabi the imagination is so important that in him we find an authentic ontology of the transcendental imagination, which means the creation of a figurative philosophy. This should not surprise us, since the imagination in its relationship to the intellect is personalized and takes the figure of the angel. The imagination and its contents provide the most explicit proof that it is legitimate to speak of a metaphysical pluralism in Ibn 'Arabi.

As we have stated, the speculative mysticism of Ibn 'Arabi is rich in determinations. For example, there are Names, presences, attributes, images, limits *(bárzaj),*[10] words, and diagrams with mathematical and cosmological references. Let us not forget that creative imagination and Soul of the World are comparable as to their ontological function, and ever since Plato wrote *Timaeus* the Soul has been determined as the sphere of mathematical ideas. However, in Ibn 'Arabi there is a figure with an especially abundant symbolism. We refer to the Universal Human *(al Insan al Kamil).* The idea of the Universal or Perfect Human (that is, the archetypal human) is linked to the category that historians and phenomenologists of religion call *protohuman.* Its variants include Gayomard, Prajapati, Adam Kadmon, Metratron, etc., and as early as Saint Paul, Christ receives the symbolic attributes of the protohuman. All these represent the notion of primordial and original human; the human fullness or the platonic idea of humanity (this is the sense of the original or heavenly man of Philo of Alexandria). In Ibn 'Arabi it also means the most complete determination of the theophanic manifestation, which means that the ineffable One is essentially self-determined by means of its human characteristics. And the reverse is also true: the subject recognizes its own substantiality in the highest and fullest plane of divine revelation. The Universal Human is, therefore, the maximum actualization and determination of the One. It is possible to affirm that the Universal Human is the best exponent of figurative philosophy by being the figure par excellence.[11] Here we also appreciate the biunity between the Creator and the creature that is reflected in the image of Universal Human, an authentic synthesis of the world of images.

In addition, it is interesting that in Swedenborg we find a figure of an extraordinary phenomenological similarity with the Universal Human of Ibn 'Arabi: the Great Human *(homo maximus)* of *Secrets of Heaven.*

The comparison is inevitable. In fact, even while recognizing the obvious differences, one cannot help but recognize that we are facing two variants of the same symbolic category. In Swedenborg the Great Human signifies the archetype or model of humanity, the effective realization of all human possibilities. In the case of the Nordic, the Great Human likewise has strong theological implications (it could be no less in an author with the religious characteristics of Swedenborg): the Great Human represents heaven, Christ, or the communion of saints.[12] It answers theological problems that always plagued Swedenborg and that can be understood from the general context of his work. What is interesting is that he uses a traditional symbol to resolve the issues that arise from that set of problems. Yet in the Prophet of the North there is another tendency that surfaces constantly: the role played by his scientific thought. The Great Human also includes the sense of *regnum animale,* the kingdom of the soul, the natural world, the physiology of the human body animated by the vital impulse, a synthesis of the spiritual and natural spheres.[13] However, what interests us most here is seeing how Swedenborg appeals to the figurative sphere to describe ideas and concepts that could not be expressed any other way. Consciousness in Swedenborg, as in Ibn 'Arabi, does not unfold only in the intellectual or conceptual sphere, but rather in inner experience, where emotion and representation are continually present in the development of the themes addressed.

The splendid system of symbols and representations that is Ibn 'Arabi's cosmos means that he cannot be considered a thinker of absolute identity or of monism, or a defender of the indeterminate and apophatic. On the contrary, everything leads us to think of Ibn 'Arabi as a philosopher of ontological determination and of substantial pluralism. The profusion of symbols, figures, and representations lead us to a coherent picture of Ibn 'Arabi as creating and sustaining a mysticism of the expressible and a figurative metaphysics.

So then what place does the Unity of Being (*Uadat al Uuyud*), which claims to be the most genuine Akbarian doctrine, occupy? Nothing we have stated until now contradicts this doctrine, since the Unity does not signify the dissolving of differences, but simply its condition of possibility. The real Unity (*Ahadiyya*) is perfect simplicity, not a numerical accumulation. This real Unity is in tension with the plurality of determinations that manifest and reveal it. The binomials Unity/Plurality and Hidden/Manifest are ways of expressing ontological differences, the presence of an absence that allows everything to be present. There is neither contradiction nor exclusion, but rather relationship and polar tension, dialectic and alternation between the One and the other.

Let us recapitulate. We have posited a comparison between Ibn 'Arabi and Swedenborg in terms of the use of symbols, representations, and similar points of view. Both participate in a personal and personalizing experience of philosophical categories, an experience that we do not hesitate to call existential because of its profound vital implications. The ontology of both is not resolved through concepts and categories, but rather through figures and representations that follow the flows of consciousness and adapt to them. In the case of Ibn 'Arabi this has the consequence of allowing us to consider him as a thinker and mystic of the pluralism of Being and of personal determination (which is evidently valid for Swedenborg also). For us, this is valuable as a general proposal about reality. In this sense Ibn 'Arabi and Swedenborg present themselves to us as prototypical authors of certain approaches and attitudes that are consistent both in their distance from purely intellectual positions and in their characteristics that are similar to a visionary hallucination: both would agree with Naser-e Khosraw's plan of the intersection of the two wisdoms; both are authors who posit the intrinsic value of the figure as a vehicle of philosophical and theological determination; and both are authors who propose a religiosity based on the concretization of personal images and representations, far from the vacuum of indetermination.

Of course, we have not exhausted the possibilities that Ibn 'Arabi and Swedenborg provide us, but our intention is to clarify the horizons that they open up for us based on the same possibilities found in figurative philosophy.

Philosophy and Homeopathy: The Influence of Swedenborg

The relationship between philosophy and medicine is a phenomenon seen continually throughout the history of ideas. Contrary to what some think, however, this relationship has not impeded the development of medical practice at all, but on the contrary has facilitated and sustained medical practice. Philosophy has supplied medicine with the theoretical model necessary to expand a system that has been rooted in pure empiricism. We see this with the Hippocratic corpus, which utilizes pre-Socratic philosophical conceptions as a vehicle or conceptual framework into which diverse medical theories can fit. Thus, concepts and categories such as the struggle of opposites, quadripartite division of natural elements, knowledge of like attracting like, and the physis are understood in a dynamic and energetic sense. All this decisively tempered the birth of medicine in ancient Greece. Certainly the Hippocratic corpus itself also influenced Greek metaphysics, but this only confirms the intimate connection between philosophy and medicine. An example of this is found in the fact that the great philosophers have also been physicians—Alcmaeon of Croton, Empedocles, Avicenna, Averroes, Maimonides, Paracelsus, etc.—and also in that many philosophical categories (the above-mentioned among them) have been present in these same theoretical bases of medicine, such as analogy and likeness among all elements of reality (in other words, the accommodation between macrocosm and microcosm), hylozoism and vitalistic organicism, etc. In summary, philosophy provides a conceptual paradigm that serves as a reference for medicine to organize and systematize experience.

The conceptual paradigms that have served medicine have been pre-Socratic metaphysics, Platonism, Aristotelianism, hermeticism, alchemy, etc. Swedenborg has also served as a theoretical paradigm for a certain type of medicine. But before continuing with this topic, let us discuss the significance of Swedenborg's thought.

Emanuel Swedenborg was an enormous influence in Romantic *Naturphilosophie* and in Romanticism in general. The reason for this influence is that the authors and thinkers of Romanticism saw in Swedenborg's ideas precisely what they desired—fundamentally, the experience of the unity and totality of reality. In fact, Romanticism is an ideological current that dramatically lives the modern Western split between the I and the not-I, between interiority and exteriority. Therefore, Romantics would be likely to look for theoretical and vital support in those systems that avoid the split of consciousness and provide, on the contrary, a globalized vision of reality in which humans find themselves in solidarity with the rest of the world. Swedenborg served Romantics well, because his thought came forth in great measure as a reaction to the dichotomies that the Enlightenment and Cartesian philosophy (though Swedenborg was an eminent representative of these philosophies during the first stage of his life) introduced in human beings and in reality as a whole: body/soul, faith/reason, matter/spirit, God/world, etc. All of Swedenborg's work—after his existential crisis of 1743–44—is directed toward overcoming the conflicts that all those dualities, and many more, imposed onto reality.

In Swedenborg's theological work there is, then, the intention to reconcile the dualities of science and religion, heaven and earth, spirit and matter, etc., in an overriding unity. To accomplish this, Swedenborg will employ all those categories that signify a holistic conception, integrating the diverse determinations of existence in a differentiated unity: analogy, correspondences, organicism, teleologism, the theory of degrees and series, etc. These will be some of the most important aspects of Swedenborg thought.

Let us now turn to homeopathy. To some degree homeopathy answers considerations that are very similar to those of *Naturphilosophie* or the Romantic philosophy of nature, since the theoretical basis of homeopathy lies in the idea of connecting the human being with totality. Regarding regional ontology, homeopathy normalizes the signs of humans with the signs of being. In this vein, it is not strange that eminent physicians who made history in homeopathy were in turn great Swedenborgians, as in the case of Constantine Hering and James Tyler Kent, among many others. We enter now into this particular aspect. We will summarize our thesis by stating that Swedenborg has served as a theoretical and systematic sustenance for medical practice. Specifically, Swedenborg's theory of degrees and series is what serves as a model and paradigm for the homeopathic doctrine, especially that of Kent. We have all read in the prologue of *Lectures on Homeopathic Philosophy* that Kent's thought is based on Samuel Hahnemann and Swedenborg.

Let us briefly explain, then, Swedenborg's doctrine of degrees. He formulates his theory of degrees and series (related to the doctrine of correspondences) as a way of obtaining a unitary vision of all orders of reality, while at the same time respecting the substantiality of those orders. Swedenborg divides reality, in a universal and hierarchical manner, into three grand spheres (degrees) that act analogically (in correspondence) in all the orders of being. Some examples of this tripartite division are:

Soul–mind–body
End–cause–effect
Love–wisdom–use
Volition–intelligence–affection
Love–faith–action
Animal–vegetable–mineral
Soul–reason–imagination
Singular–particular–general
Superior–middle–inferior
Inmost–internal–external

In each of these triads of degrees, the first entity is superior from the metaphysical point of view, that is, in an ontological hierarchy; the second entity signifies the middle term of the scale; and the third entity is the inferior and most superficial. In this theory of degrees, applicable to everything, Swedenborg introduces a fundamental fact: the degrees are communicable and are open to divine influx, which thus penetrates everything. By referring to the opening of the degrees, Swedenborg means to say that the orders of reality do not form self-contained compartments, but rather they belong to a greater structure that connects and determines them. For this reason Swedenborg's theory of degrees can also be configured in the following way: Swedenborg divided the series of these degrees into two classes, the degrees of height and those of width. The degrees of height are successive and discrete (that is, separated); they go from greater to lesser if they begin from above, or from the lesser to the greater if they begin from below. The degrees of width are simultaneous and continuous, and they go from the interior to the exterior. Swedenborg offers the example of a column divided into three sections: the highest, the middle, and the lowest (the degrees of height); and in addition each section of the column would have three continuous degrees of width: inmost, interior or middle, and exterior. There is a correspondence between the highest and the inmost, between the middle and the interior, and between the lowest and the exterior. All instantiation that is found in a degree of height participates at the same time in a determined degree of width. All degrees of height being in communication, everything becomes a receptacle of the higher orders. Thus arrive Divinity, Infinity, Truth, and Good to all and each one of the orders, including the lowest ones.

Let us return now to James Tyler Kent. It is evident that the theory of degrees is present in his *Lectures on Homeopathic Philosophy* and in all his medical thought. For Kent, the cause of illness is the disunity of understanding and volition in humans, and this imbalance would manifest itself in use and in effects, that is, the exteriority that reveals the action of understanding and volition.

The cure, according to Kent, always goes from top to bottom (degrees of height) and from inside out (degrees of width). That is, the curative potential follows the order of communication of the degrees (see lecture 2, paragraph c in the above-referenced book).

Knowledge of the principles that govern the human being is indispensable for correct therapy. Those governing principles in humans are triadic: brain/cerebellum/spinal cord; volition/understanding/vital force. The body is differentiated into interior, center, and exterior (lecture 4).

The interior forms the exterior. The order goes from the highest to the lowest, from the center to the circumference (lecture 5).

The importance of influx as a vital force and simple substance lies in the fact that it transmits its *vis formativa* (formative force), its finality and utility, to all parts of the human being by means of degrees (lecture 8). In a similar fashion, the vital dynamism of medicinal substances attains the whole series of potencies, since the substances are receptacles of that same vital dynamism. The causes continue in the effects (lecture 14).

In all these Kentian proposals, extracted from *Lectures on Homeopathic Philosophy*, Swedenborg's influence makes itself clear, especially the theory of degrees. By means of this theory, Kent could explain the curative action of the medications independently of quantitative factors. There being a certain homogeneity among all the orders of reality, curative dynamics effect their influence by means of all those orders. It is evident, then, that the Swedenborgian presence in Kent is general, since he shares the fundamental principles of Swedenborg's system: a unitary and holistic conception of reality, correspondence of all the spheres of existence, vital organicism, teologism, etc. One of the applications made by Kent affects the notion of correspondence, and we can legitimately consider that the *Repertory of the Homeopathic Materia Medica* is designed as a type of grandiose *clavis* or key (let us not forget that one of Swedenborg's books was *Clavis Hieroglyphica [Hieroglyphic Key]*) where correspondences are established between people, symptoms, infirmities, and medications. Swedenborg certainly influenced Kent's scientific and theoretical work (Swedenborg's theory of degrees, developed in his theological stage, is an internalization of the anatomical ideas developed in the book *Oeconomia Regni Animalis,* which belongs to the scientific stage). However, Swedenborg's religious aspects also had a strong influence on Kent (as they did on many other homeopathic physicians), since Kent was a faithful adherent of the New Church, as were many other famous homeopaths, such as James John Garth Wilkinson (one of the first translators of Swedenborg into English), Constantine Hering, Otis Clapp, Hans Gram, John Ellis, Henry James, etc.

The figure of James Tyler Kent seems to us paradigmatic, as he demonstrates the utilization of a certain theoretical model of medical practice. If Kent turns to Swedenborg, it is because the Swede provided him with the conceptual elements needed to organize the *materia medica* into a coherent system. Yet above all, what Kent reveals is the way that Swedenborg's visions unite and interpenetrate with those of Samuel Hahnemann, undoubtedly due to the fact that both respond to common assumptions and motivations.

Finally, we want to emphasize once more that a philosophical—and even theological—conception is not necessarily an obstacle for medical theories and practices. On the contrary, a philosophical model can provide internal coherence to medicine. We believe that Kent demonstrates this explicitly with respect to Swedenborg's work and doctrine.

10

SWEDENBORG AND ROMANTIC
RELIGIOSITY

Undoubtedly all who have approached the figure of Emanuel Swedenborg have seen the enormous influence of the Swedish thinker on Romanticism, and more specifically on what we could call the Romantic religious consciousness.[1] Therefore, it is pertinent to explain the possible causes of this Swedenborgian presence in the Romantic experience of the sacred as we penetrate the modes and forms through which that religious ideology was expressed. Above all, we feel the need to establish a framework that would help to clarify the motives behind the Romantic acceptance of Swedenborgian ideas. The lines of thought that move through the European modern age and flourish in Romanticism, thus determining its religiosity, can be synthesized in the following manner:

A) After the Reformation there is an incessant movement of consciousness that yearns for a more spiritual and profound experience of Christianity.[2] The Protestant Reformation, consolidated through the creation of new churches that were more visible and embraced a new set of laws, did not quench the thirst for free spirituality of those who aspired to an unmediated, direct relationship with Divinity. The mysticism that arose from the areas that embraced the Reformation, as well as Spanish mysticism in the Catholic sphere, need to be understood as a manifestation of this phenomenon. The second Reformation or Radical Reformation signifies another attempt at reaching the pristine state of a pure and original Christianity. But the impulse toward religious renovation, internalization, and spiritualization that began with the modern age has still neither culminated nor completed for the individuals who are most demanding in terms of their own life experience, a situation that produces a lack of confidence in all institutional churches. One thus sees the beginnings of the idea of a Church of Saint John versus a Church of Saint Peter, where the Church of Saint John would be an inner church, invisible, without worship nor clergy, to which all those who were left unsatisfied by institutionalized religion belonged. Ultimately, the Church of Saint John is a universal church, since its foundation is based on the innermost consciousness and not on rules and external laws, and the essence of the human soul is the same everywhere. (This idea is associated with a belief that will pave the way for a unique and original Revelation for all humanity.) On the other hand, the Church of Saint Peter represents the external and visible aspects of Christianity, where worship and normative religiosity occur. The Church of Saint Peter is certainly necessary to the degree in which it satisfies the religiosity of a majority of the faithful (it is thus an exoteric church). Additionally, the Church of Saint Peter fulfills the role of guarantor of social order, while the inner, spiritual church (the Church of Saint John) enters into conflict with the trappings of external piety and becomes imbued with anti-clericalism (more or less pronounced, more or less subtle). The development of modern, revolutionary utopianism is inseparable from the unleashing of esoteric ideas related to millennialism, to such an extent that we can affirm that, in a certain measure, chiliasm has been assimilated by all esoteric and theosophical currents. These, in turn, stimulated by a deep spiritual anxiety and desire for effective social justice, have generated a great many of the modern revolutionary doctrines.

B) Another important phenomenon for our topic is a tradition of esoteric and Spiritualist persuasion that continues throughout the modern age. Beginning with the Renaissance a there is a desire to connect with the initial and primordial chain, which in fact produces a revival—if not an authentic creation—of esoteric currents. At times these materialize in the figure of the secret society, the alleged preserver of an arcane and primordial knowledge. Let us not forget that the exhumation and rediscovery of texts carried out during the Renaissance (the corpus of hermetic texts) has aided the formation of this type of spirituality. Disciplines such as alchemy or the kabbalah (reinterpreted according to the new times) form a part of the genesis of the esoteric spirituality of the modern era.[3] All this, as we have stated, generally has the secret society or brotherhood as its vehicle: Rosicrucianism, Elus Cohens, Masonry, etc. The secret society thus often becomes a refuge for those spirits who cannot satisfy their piety in the official churches, yielding to the mutual benefit of the inward-focused attitudes of the above-named Church of Saint John and the fellowship of those souls who seek a more profound Christian experience in esotericism and the secret society. In short, the religious and sociological sphere of the occult brotherhood will become the characteristic of the invisible church, since esotericism itself brings about mystical religiosity, and, vice versa, a religiosity at the margins of established religion finds its natural place in a more or less esoteric or confraternal environment.[4]

C) An idea that has developed throughout the modern age is that of an original and universal Revelation from which all religions emerged. Its language would be expressed in traditional symbols, in popular legends, in mythology, in poetry—in short, in language itself. The consequences of this idea of original Revelation will be crucial, because so many spheres of thought will be affected by it, and also because it will be the determining factor in the development of those spheres. We are referring to the issue of original language, an issue associated with the idea of primordial Revelation.[5] In fact, we need to place speculations about the origin of language within this order of things—what traces or footprints might remain of the pristine sacred language and what such a language could have been like, a language identified, as we have stated, with the most primitive Revelation made by God to human beings. This revealed language would adopt multiple forms, and there would be privileged places in which the presence of the original words reflect more density: poetry would be one of those privileged places, because it would normally would be united to speculations about primordial language and poetical works.[6] In addition, there are other reflections of this language, more or less veiled (Orientalism plays a fundamental role in this sense): the esoteric tradition (which establishes itself as the most suitable vehicle of transmission and interpretation), poetry, and popular literature. A genre is born in this respect, the *clavis hieroglyphica,* attempting to provide the universal interpretive key capable of deciphering the set of signs, symbols, and emblems (the hieroglyphs) that compose the universal fabric of revealed meaning. Any field of experience may form part of this fabric: poetry, theology, biblical exegesis, art, sciences, and so on—we find all their symbols being interrelated.[7] The interpretations of this universal language adopt multiple aspects and variants: the universal language (generally connected with the idea of Revelation or pristine origin) can be poetry, music, dreams, symbols of nature, myths, or even concrete languages: Hebrew, Sanskrit, Chinese, Spanish, etc.

Naturally, the idea of Revelation is reinforced in turn by the existence of esoteric societies or brotherhoods, which fulfill the functions of transmitting and holding back the content of the Revelation, and because of this the idea of primordial and universal Revelation is inseparable from the idea of Tradition. This introduces many nuances necessary to outline the relationship between Revelation and Tradition from the perspective of the esoteric and mystical society. Generally, there is a golden chain that keeps the revealed tradition alive and also creates a carrier for the interpretation of the hieroglyphs in which tradition is manifested. Clearly the Christians who belong to the mystical church or the Church of Saint John will become part of the golden chain of seers and transmitters of that original Revelation.

As can be shown, there are some cross-references that connect the representatives and tendencies of the three groups we have cited, and so we will need to keep in mind these three groups, together with their interrelations, when it comes time to explain the fundamental concepts of Romantic religiosity. Naturally, we find other factors that also contribute to what will come to be the religious sentiment of Romanticism. Among all those factors, we would like to mention the following, for their importance: First, scientism that is increasingly mixed with esotericism, which will result in occultism in a strict sense. Another of those elements consists of the feeling of social revolution that often accompanies the Spiritualist and esoteric currents to which we have been referring; this revolutionary sentiment, when united with the other trends cited, becomes a plan for a total revolution (palingenesis) that includes eschatological tendencies.[8] There is a dialectical relationship between the esoteric currents and the spiritual reformative expectations that conclude in Romanticism, giving place to its own religious experience. On one hand, those esoteric currents feed the needs of unsatisfied souls by means of contact with the supernatural.[9] On the other hand, those same spiritual expectations created ways of experiencing the sacred: esotericism itself, and many of its forms and categories. So we have, for example, the secret society, and we also have the kabbalah, which provides a mystical and personal method of access to the veiled meaning of the Bible, ultimately making it so that one derives the ideas of restorative and reactivating hermeneutics of meaning from this type of experience (since this is precisely the aim of the kabbalah).[10]

Together with these ideological lines, which continued unfolding throughout the modern age and which produced Romantic religiosity, we find another ideology that is more extensive and general, like a constant that frames all of them. We refer to the search for a unifying vision of reality by means of which the split in consciousness—especially Romantic consciousness—is resolved and overcome. That is, it is a matter of reaching a synthesis that can overcome the dichotomies of infinity and finite, visible and visible, the I and the not-I. Certainly all religious experience tends to annul the differences between the Absolute and the particular, but this tendency is accentuated as we approach Romanticism. This is due to the parallel development of another ideological line, one which is distinguished by having broken the ties between individuality and Totality, while isolating it from any relationship with Unity in order to reduce it to its immanent sphere. Thus, Romanticism desires not only a connection of the subject with the Absolute, but also a knowledge of totality—that is, a knowledge in which one focuses on the particular from the perspective of the whole, and that whole is reflected in each particular. The fragmentation of knowledge is a correlate of the fragmentation of the world, and hence the profusion of works that aim to have encyclopedic knowledge, or that give an account of origins (origins of language, of religion, or of Revelation itself), or those that want to provide the ultimate interpretive key to all of reality. These are books and systems that seek to reduce the plurality to its essential unity, in the same way that split consciousness aspires to connection with the All. Unity is posited as a supreme category that needs to govern reality: a universal language, a universal religion, a unitary vision of the world. Thus it was in the time of origins, and thus it should be once again. We can thus establish a new cross-reference between this last aspect and all the former ones. We can summarize this description of defining parameters of Romantic religiosity thus: consciousness of infinity, of the absolute, and of the universal results in a preference for the occult and esoteric, for Dream and Night. Other aspects can be added: universal symbolism, religious syncretism, an organic vision of nature (*Naturphilosophie,* alchemy), etc. We believe that these brief shared notes are sufficient to frame the religious sentiment of Romanticism in its relationship with Swedenborg.

Let us return, then, to Swedenborg. We need to say first that we must differentiate very clearly between the genuine Swedenborg and the interpretation that the Romantics made of the wise Swede. Our thesis consists in affirming that those large sections (A–C) seen earlier as central tenets of Romantic religiosity are applied by Romantics to Swedenborg's ideas, and the result is a strange and particular Swedenborg, one perfectly adapted to the spiritual anxieties, desires, and necessities of Romanticism. Summing up, the Romantic perspective that contemplates the work of Swedenborg generates a vision of him that in great measure is a distortion, but that ultimately is one that influences the makeup of Romantic religiosity.

Before examining how the Romantic reception of Swedenborg came about, taking into account the diverse aspects we have cited, we will attempt to synthesize what could be the fundamental points of Swedenborg's thought. Two, in our judgment, stand out above all the rest. First of all is the essential characteristic that stems from Swedenborg's scientific background in relation to his questions regarding faith: In this sense Swedenborg presents himself to us as the prototype of the Enlightenment scientist who wants to encompass the religious vision of the world within that same scientific horizon. That is, he posits a conception where there is no gap between reason and faith, science and spirituality; he tries to resolve all the dualities that split the consciousness of modern humans. His method consists of extrapolating scientific laws to the spiritual sphere and of showing the continuity between both realities. Thus, it is very important to be familiar with Swedenborg's scientific work in order to understand his theological work. Swedenborg represents the total system, the total book, and the total code (Romantics will especially appreciate this aspect of unity and totality coinciding).

The other fundamental point of Swedenborg's thought lies in its specifically Christian characteristics; more concretely, the preeminence that Swedenborg concedes to works versus faith, to free will versus bound will (with the consequent confrontation with Lutheranism). We need to place another essential characteristic of Swedenborg in this category: the role that biblical exegesis plays throughout the Scandinavian's works. We could even affirm that his entire body of work is a hermeneutic leading to the discovery of inner meaning and to experience that veiled (and transmitted) meaning through the literal meaning.[11]

Scientific training, the urge for Christian reform, the desire for a unitary vision of reality, the inner experience and spiritual exegesis of the Bible: here we have a summary of the substance of Swedenborg's thought, to which we would need to add—since it would be very important for the Romantic mentality—the form of exposition of this thought; it is carried out by means of visions in which angelology performs a very important role.

If we connect the central tenets of Romanticism with those of similar vein in Swedenborgianism, we will arrive at the Romantic's ideas about Swedenborg, especially in relation to religious sentiment. We will also be able to appreciate the differences between the true Swedenborgian issues and the interpretations made by the Romantics. In any case, what seems clear to us is what we will attempt to show, which is the influence of Swedenborg on the shape of Romantic religious thought and feeling.

For many Romantics Emanuel Swedenborg proved to be the prototypical figure who symbolized their own spiritual longings. Consequently, the Prophet of the North was one of the people on the list of saints of esoteric thought, and, in our case, Romantic thought. In fact, we will see how Swedenborg answers all the assumptions we have mentioned. He includes himself within the category of Christian reformers that attempt and posit a more internalized, purified, lived Christian experience. In some ways this is the fundamental motivation of his work: the critique of Lutheran formalism and of the external aspects of Catholicism, and the positing of a discovery of inner biblical meaning as a source of true Christian experience. All this is summarized in Swedenborg in a return to pre-Nicean Christianity, which according to him is the most authentic and pure. As can be shown, the necessary conditions exist for Romanticism to see Swedenborg as a leading representative of the Church of Saint John or interior church to which we referred earlier. There are other factors that help facilitate this tendency, the principal one being the consideration of Swedenborg as a member of the esoteric tradition and of that golden chain of mystical transmissions. For the Romantics, the figure of the wise Swede is linked with that of Orpheus, Pythagoras, Zarathustra, Moses, Agrippa, Paracelsus, and Boehme, among others. This is due to a deficient understanding of Swedenborg's work (popularized through indirect versions or summaries),[12] which brings about the interpretation of certain elements of Swedenborg—visionary experiences, dreams, angels, and descriptions of celestial or invisible spheres—commensurately with the categories of theosophy and the occult that were much in fashion during that era. Thus Swedenborg is converted into a link in the chain of transmission of the initiatory wisdom coming from the original Revelation. Swedenborg is seen as the restorer of that pristine and arcane wisdom, serving as a prophet and seer, inaugurating a new humanity. These two positions are not contradictory, but rather it is a question of nuances.

Several themes play a key role in this consideration of Swedenborg. For example, in his books he alludes to an Ancient or Adamic Church and an original language spoken by angels (which also corresponds with the spiritual sense of the Bible). Swedenborg has various classifications of the ages of the world. The best known is: Most Ancient Church (or Adamic, the one that had the primordial language), Ancient Church (or Judaic, characterized by a worship based on analogies and representations), Christian Church, and New Church. Other, variant classifications are divided more or less as follows: the antediluvian age, the age of Asia-Africa, the Judaic age, and the Christian age. Each age or church assumes a degree of internalization, or what we could consider states of the soul (either in an individual or a collective sense). It is interesting to note that for Swedenborg, the scripture revealed to the Most Ancient Church was lost through the Fall, with only a few traces remaining in the Great Tartary. Without a doubt, this belief in a lost original Scripture in the center of Asia must have fed the Romantic zeal for Orientalism.[13]

Another theme would be the complex system of analogies, correspondences, and representations that turn our world into a network of symbols and emblems; these are connected to the invisible world and therefore maintain the material world through their transcendence. The theme of Last Judgment also appears in Swedenborg, but in his sense it means the discovery of the inner meaning of Scripture; it refers to a realized eschatology, since the Last Judgment will happen when the soul opens up in the presence of Meaning.

Other important points of Swedenborg's thought were especially susceptible to being received by the Romantics, such as the role that he gives to conjugal love.[14] However, what was most influential in our judgment was Swedenborg's scientific training and his encyclopedic knowledge. This was crucial because the theosophy in fashion (actually an occultism) had a scientific element, or more precisely an element of scientism, and Swedenborg fulfilled this requirement (as a visionary and man of science at the same time) in the eyes of the Romantics imbued with occultist ideas.[15] Swedenborg's encyclopedic knowledge is clearly framed within the Romantic's desire for a unitary knowledge of totality, principally through the construction of a system in which the diverse parcels of reality are assembled and connected in a globalizing vision of totality. Swedenborg's work responded to a fundamental impulse of Romanticism: overcome the split between world and consciousness, finite and infinite, visible and invisible. Therein lies the religious Romantic sentiment, and this is where Swedenborg serves to fill the needs of that religious sentiment. Certainly Swedenborg's generalizing tendency to internalize and translate all the categories of external reality (including theological categories) in terms of consciousness facilitates an interpretation of this system under the same schema in Romanticism.

Let us remember that for Swedenborg consciousness is central, and its dynamism dominates the diverse aspects of religious life, so that concepts such as heaven, hell, church, etc., are converted into flows, movements, and states of the soul. As Swedenborg puts it: "Divinity in the whole heaven and Divinity in an individual angel is the same. This is why all heaven can be seen as a single angel. The same holds true for the church and for the individual member of it" (*Divine Love and Wisdom* §79); "[T]he spiritual world is right where we are, not distanced from us in the least" (§92).

There are other factors the facilitate the Romantic vision of Swedenborg: the presence of angels and ecstatic visions and experiences throughout his works make it especially suitable for assimilation by occultist currents, although all those experiences occupy a very different place in his thought than they do in occultism.[16]

However, the profound differences between Swedenborg and Romantic ideology have not been hidden from anyone. For Romantics, Swedenborg was an instrument to access the Absolute; centered on their specific issues, the Romantics failed to recognize—or deliberately distorted—the true perspective from which the Prophet of the North should be contemplated: as an enlightened wise man who desires an exhaustive knowledge of all orders of reality, as a religious man who aspires to a profound experience of Christianity, and as a human figure who attempts a coherent and systematized interrelation between those two aspects.

Let us now examine some of the differences between Swedenborg and Romanticism. First of all, we need to clarify that Swedenborg does not affiliate himself with any spiritual, mystical, or esoteric movement. It is possible that phenomenologically there are Swedenborgian themes and motifs that might coincide with those of Romanticism, but the specific importance of his doctrine is a response to distinct antecedents and to a distinct intellectual tradition. Descartes, Malebranche, Leibniz, Wolff, and the scientific thought of his era helped to form Swedenborg's ideas, rather than thinkers like Paracelsus, Kircher, Boehme, Guyon, Saint Teresa, Molinos, or Schwenckfeld (whom he tends to ignore). This does not mean that there are no phenomenological connections between the latter group of figures and those with whom

Swedenborg affiliates; this happens because of similar shared issues, experiences, and answers.

A phenomenological approach that compares Spanish mysticism and Swedenborg's experiences would not be insignificant, since they both obey impulses of an emotive and perceptible religiosity rather than a conceptual or noetic impulse of the neoplatonic mode. Undoubtedly the Hernnhutist influence on the Swedish thinker helped to determine his religious experience as far as giving priority to the effects of his perceptions. That influence played an important role in the totality of Swedenborg's work, with its representative and figurative tone. Swedenborg can be likened to Saint John of the Cross or Saint Teresa in his motifs of love, proactivity, or the image of Christ crucified as a driving force for inner transformation. Swedenborg states thus: "'Fearing God' means fearing to offend him, and sinning is offending him. This really comes from love rather than from fear. If we love others, are we not afraid of hurting them? The more we love them, the greater the fear" (*Divine Providence* §140).

These words, by their tone and content, are perfectly comparable with that superb anonymous sonnet: "I am not moved to love you, Lord." Therefore, it makes sense to affiliate the following thinkers existentially and in a personalist manner: Saint John of the Cross, Saint Teresa, Hamann, Swedenborg, Kierkegaard, Unamuno, Berdyaev, and so on. Obviously this mystical aspect of Swedenborg is a determining factor in the Romantic reception of his work, since Romanticism tends to prioritize elements that lead to categories of living, feeling, inner experience, etc. (without a doubt the constitution of generalized hermeneutics is similar).

Another affiliation one can make with our author is the one presented by Regis Boyer in the prologue to his translation of Swedenborg's *Journal of Dreams* (Paris, 1985): Ibsen, Strindberg, Kierkegaard, Lagerkvist (and we would add Saint Bridget, Almqvist, and Ekelöf, among others). He sees a Nordic affiliation, wanting to demonstrate a certain unity of attitudes characteristic of the Scandinavian culture. Along the same lines, Eric Peterson associates our author with Kierkegaard and states insightfully: "It is better, perhaps, to remember a vision of Swedenborg, the other great critic, with Kierkegaard, of Scandinavian Protestantism. In a room without doors and windows, the Protestant preacher walks back and forth, always repeating the same words: 'sola fide.' This vision, which posits in an extraordinary manner the monotony of the Protestant rhetoric that emanates from nominalism, is the foundation of all pietistic criticism of Protestant orthodoxy."[17] In any case, this unity would be given by an existential tension toward transcendence and by an introspection in the abyss of the consciousness, which would coincide with the affiliation that we proposed.

Another characteristic that impedes placing Swedenborg within the esoteric line (as did the Romantics of theosophic persuasion) lies in the fact that there is no process of initiation of any kind in Swedenborgian doctrine. In fact, for Swedenborg his visionary experiences are a response to a crisis of faith and are completely free and personal. There is no process of initiation for such experiences at all; they are not applicable to just anyone, that is, no one can repeat the very same spiritual experiences that Swedenborg lived purely by divine grace. This point is perhaps the one that most clearly signals the difference between Swedenborg and the Romantic interpretation of him.

Neither did the wise Swede belong to any sect, lodge, or brotherhood, nor did he have any intention of creating one. The appropriations of Swedenborg's name made by the Illuminati of Avignon, Masonry, or any other society have no basis in his life and work. Not even the Church of the New Jerusalem is a result of any direct action of Swedenborg, but rather of his followers.

In addition, Swedenborg's doctrine does not present millenarian, palingenetic, or social reformist traits, as is found in Romantic esoteric visions (the Romantic hero is a mix of initiate, prophet, and revolutionary). In contrast, Swedenborg's ideas of the Last Judgment and of the Apocalypse are better framed within what we might call fulfilled eschatology (although there are certainly ethical motivations in Swedenborg), based on the discovery of the spiritual sense of the Bible and in its internalization. In this way, all of Swedenborg's work is resolved in a conversion of external instantiations into interiorist, personalist, and proactive terms, with which we obtain a system where the categories of love prevail over those of knowledge. Swedenborg's doctrine is clearly distanced from the occultist coloring of theosophic theories and consequently from the interpretation the theosophic Romantics made of Swedenborg.

In short, there is a Swedenborg linked to theosophism, mesmerism, and esoteric tendencies, which is the Romantic interpretation of the Scandinavian theologian. There is also the genuine Swedenborg, who is characterized by an existential conception conducive to an internal, personalized, and individualized experience of Christianity together with a unified vision of reality in its totality. What is certain is that Swedenborg's doctrine provided Romantic religiosity with a mystical longing for infinity set within a coherent system of degrees of being, of analogies, and of correspondences, although the differences are clearly visible. Perhaps the acerbic criticism William Blake made of Swedenborg in *The Marriage of Heaven and Hell* reflects this irreconcilable separation between the Romantic perspective (Blake's, to be precise) and the more specific doctrine of Swedenborg. Do we not find paradigmatic this very difference in the Romantic nocturnal focus represented by a Novalis versus the diurnal focus common to the theories and visions of Swedenborg? There are multiple Swedenborgian themes interpreted in their own manner by diverse Romantic authors. For example, the recurrence of the androgyne myth in Romanticism leads Romantics to interpret Swedenborg's writings on conjugal love based on that myth. This is an evident distortion of the ideas and intentions of the Prophet of the North, for whom the continuity of love between spouses entails a stronger insistence on the personalizing and individualizing factors of his thought. In contrast, the myth of the androgyne implies a dissolving of the members of the pair. In general terms we can affirm that one of the fundamental attractions that Romantic religiosity feels for Swedenborg lies in the personalizing and determined character that abstract theological categories adopt in the doctrine of the wise Swede. This makes it especially attractive to poets, artists, and thinkers who are more representative than conceptual (and let us not forget that religiosity is always representative and imaginative, versus abstract and conceptual theology).[18]

We have briefly seen the assumptions that explain the presence of Swedenborg in the configuration of Romantic religiosity. Certain elements of Swedenborg's doctrine give rise to the sacred aspect of the

Romantic phenomenon; the Romantic phenomenon raises the presence of Swedenborgian elements by virtue of its own needs and religious longings. It is not, then, simply a genetic relationship.

The sphere opened through this fusion of horizons is what characterizes the Romantic religious sentiment: desire for infinity, priority of inwardness, the symbolic relationship between the different states of reality, a globalizing vision of the whole, and finally, the search for the Absolute that is represented as the Arcane, the Supernatural, the Mystery, the Origin, and so on. All those modes are inherent to the Romantic experience of the soul, as a consciousness of its separation and as aspirations of unity.

We repeat again: Swedenborg serves as a vehicle for the exposition of all these Romantic ideas. Ultimately, what lies behind these complex systems of symbolisms, representations, and correspondences is the feeling of harmony and of consciousness with the world and with God. And in this Swedenborg and the Romantic religiosity coincide.

In an article by Michel Deneken titled "Les Romantiques allemands, promoteurs de la notion d'eglise sacrement de salut?" ("German Romantics: Promoters of the Notion of Church as Sacrament of Salvation?")[19] Romantic religiosity is discussed in a certain way with some terms which are very similar to ours. In this article Deneken speaks of the constitution of the theological category of "church as sacrament of salvation" from the perspective of the experiences and speculations of German Romantics who thought about the church as an inner sphere and internalizer of consciousness (without diminishing, naturally, the fact that the notion has its most pristine origin in the idea of "mystical body"). To establish his study the author comments on J. G. Hamann, J. K. Lavater, Jung-Stilling, J. G. Herder, F. Jacobi, and Goethe. Throughout all of this, in a succinct but illuminating analysis, Deneken discovers all the elements (those which we have discussed before) that generate or make possible the idea of Church as sacrament: the Bible and the world considered as a symbolic system that we must unveil; the presence of the invisible in the visible; generalized internalization; an interest in everything Original (language, religion, poetry, hieroglyphics) as a common patrimony of humanity; and, finally, a search for Unity in all the orders of reality. All this leads, as Deneken sees quite well, to the positing of an inner church (*sacramentum salutis*) as an ideal of the Romantic spirituality. In fact, the church as sacrament of salvation is the consequence of the entire process of internalization that the religiosity of Romanticism entails. All these factors are the same ones that we have shown to be fundamental to Romantic spirituality when we were relating all those elements to Romanticism's reception of Swedenborg.

The conclusion that we would reach, then, would be that Swedenborg's ideas occupy a crucial place in the Romantic constitution of the category of Church as sacrament, given that Swedenborg himself was a driving force behind the idea and experience of the inner Church, in line with his system as a whole. Deneken, however, does not name Swedenborg in his article, in spite of the fact that we recognize the influence of the wise Swede in some of the figures alluded to. Specifically, Deneken does not taken into account Lavater, Jung-Stilling, and Goethe (in his novel *Elective Affinities*), in addition to other thinkers within this same order of things.

There is another issue we would like to address. The category church as sacrament of salvation is a response to the Romantic need for interiority. But (and this also is very well expressed by Deneken) together with this need for internalization we find a counterpart expressed in the word sacrament. That is to say, we have the idea of sacramentality as symbol, visible sign, and externalization that serves as a vehicle to the spiritual and interior world. Let us not forget that one of the driving motives of the whole Romantic religious movement lies in the criticism of the Protestant fideist dryness and the reduction of Christian life to pure ethics (which demonstrates that the symbol is innate to all religious experience). Thus the neo-sacramentalism and the neo-Catholicism of so many Romantics: F. Schlegel, Wackenroder, Tieck, Novalis, Sternbald, Baader, and so on.

In Swedenborg we find likewise the criticism of the Lutheran idea of *sola fide* and *servo arbitrio,* and against this the constant recognition of works and of free will. In addition, the theory of correspondences and representations contributes a symbolic element that connects the visible with the invisible. We find in Swedenborg the same synthesis between interiority and exteriority that later would be the principal motif of Romantic religiosity.

11

SOME REFLECTIONS *(Ex Auditis et Visis)*

In the preceding pages we have attempted to give some guidelines that will serve to approach the reading and comprehension of Swedenborg. We shall emphasize these guidelines, summarizing the ones we consider the most important, the ones that are hermeneutical keys for understanding Swedenborg's work. The ontological horizon that the keys unlock for us will help locate our author within the philosophy of religion, or within restorative hermeneutics, or within a religiously tinged existentialism. In the end, an examination of Swedenborg should respond to the same demands that he applied to reality: look for the inner meaning, the innermost depths of all things. We base one of these fundamental models of Swedenborgian thought on the meaning of interiority. Let us look at others.

The importance that the subject acquires for Swedenborg seems to us especially noteworthy. In fact, many categories of his philosophy and theology (at times expressed through mythical channels) are revealed to us as arguments and postulates that reinforce the position of the subject in the world and especially the position of the subject with respect to science. Swedenborg questions the debilitated status that the subject slowly acquired in the science of his time, and by contrast Swedenborg posits an affirmation of science and of its image of the world, but also of human beings and their most internal and qualitative aspects. Swedenborg definitely aims to reconcile interiority with exteriority (and thus the Romantic interest in our author).

Swedenborg's philosophical-theological system is a product of a radical religious experience. Therefore, the language that attempts to express such experience cannot be an ordinary language, nor can it obey an everyday logic. In some way he himself has to be a language that molds itself to that which attempts to communicate—in other words, he should consist of a radical language. The analysis of language is important for all philosophy of religion, because it denotes the experiences of religious life. In Swedenborg's case, his language turns out to be fundamental information for understanding the type of experience to which he refers and expresses. It is normal, then, that Swedenborg's work is a narrative that breaks with everyday logic, since the experience that he attempts to reveal also breaks with everyday logic. As Lars Bergquist affirms, all the great Spiritualists have expressed their inner lives in a way that assumes a rupture of the plane of existence.[1] We could affirm that a radical religious experience reinvents language, since it is of a radically different reality from what it has to express. We can think of many Spiritualists, visionaries, or mystics and we can demonstrate how their discourse assumes an interruption of their habitual discourses. However, the singular case of Swedenborg rests on the fact that while he explains his inner experiences, he sets them within a perspective that denotes his training in Enlightenment science. This is not any kind of extravagance, since for Swedenborg it is precisely a matter of establishing the accommodation between interiority and exteriority, between the invisible and the visible. Therefore, for the wise Swede there is a correlation (if not identity) between the structures of the soul and those of the world.

We have repeatedly labeled Swedenborg and his system as existential. By doing this we have wanted to make reference to an attitude, a general tone, an impulse. We have attempted to approach his thought in a manner analogous to what Hans Jonas did in his approach to gnosticism, also establishing similarities with existentialism. For us, however, this label has a positive sense rather than a negative one. When we speak of the existential in relation to Swedenborg, we want to signify, above all, his thought as the projection of consciousness toward human fullness, a projection expressed faithfully in these words: "This has led some people to believe that anything spiritual is like a bird that flies beyond the air into the ether, beyond the reach of our eyesight. In fact, though, it is like a bird of paradise flying so close to our eyes that its lovely feathers brush the pupils, willing to be seen. 'Our eyesight' means our intellectual sight" (*Divine Love and Wisdom* §374).

It could seem strange that we have not dedicated any separate chapter to Swedenborg's angelology, given the importance that the theme of angels has for the wise Swede. In fact, the role of the angels turns out to be omnipresent throughout Swedenborg's works, so that in reality any themes or issues we examine regarding our author assumes a relationship in one way or another to angelology. If we begin with Swedenborg's own religious experience, it is due to and rests on experiences related to angels, which gives Swedenborg's religiosity its own particular tenor: the experience of mediation, of representation, of the cataphatic; therefore, experience of divinity as determination (to illustrate this type of religiosity we refer again to Corbin, *L'Homme et son ange [Man and His Angel]*). In that which refers to human beings, the figure of the angel signifies the ontological status of their determination, of their fullness. The impulse that leads human beings to transcend is crystallized and articulated in the image of the angel. The personalization and the intensification of consciousness as a goal and driving force of human spiritual dynamism likewise has its regulating paradigm in the angel. Biblical exegesis, the Great Human, and the church (that is, the communitarian and collective sense of religious life) also find themselves determined by the figure of the angel; conjugal love in heaven is a variation on the gnostic theme of the syzygy between the human soul and its angel. In short, all of Swedenborg's arguments are touched upon by the wing of an angel, and thus to speak of any of these arguments means to speak of angels, since for Swedenborg angels form the dimension where events occur that specifically concern human beings. Angelology is, then, the conclusion of anthropology, the corollary of a phenomenology of meaning and of the consciousness that is opened to the epiphany of this meaning: "[T]he angels receive all their wisdom from the Word; they themselves assert this. They have as much light as they have understanding of the Word" (*True Christianity* §242).

NOTES

Unless otherwise noted, the translations of Swedenborg's works in this English edition were taken directly from the New Century Edition of the Works of Emanuel Swedenborg, published by the Swedenborg Foundation. In some cases this has resulted in differences in wording from the original Spanish citations; where the difference is substantial we have included an explanation in the notes below. Because the New Century Edition was a work in progress at the time of publication, we would like to thank the following people for providing translations of unpublished passages: Lisa Hyatt Cooper for *Secrets of Heaven;* George F. Dole for *Revelation Unveiled, Last Judgment, Sacred Scripture,* and *White Horse;* and Stuart Shotwell for *Apocalypse Explained (Revelation Explained).*

Preface

1. Karl Kerényi, *La religión antigua* (Madrid, 1972), 99.

Introduction

1. Without attempting to exhaust the list of figures influenced by Swedenborg, we will cite: William Blake, Novalis, Pierre-Simon Ballanche, Honoré de Balzac, Gérard de Nerval, Christian Johann Heinrich Heine, Friedrich Wilhelm Joseph Schelling, Charles Baudelaire, Fyodor Dostoevsky, August Strindberg, Miguel de Unamuno, Oscar and Czeslaw Milosz, Ralph Waldo Emerson, Eugeni d'Ors, Jorge Luis Borges, etc.

2. This issue has been treated analytically and thoroughly by Karl-Erik Sjöden in *Swedenborg en France* (Stockholm: Almquist-Wiksell, 1985) and in "On French Swedenborgianism," *Studia Scandinavica* 10 (1988): 63–73.

3. "There is inner compulsion and inner freedom. Inner compulsion is found in people who are busy with outward worship alone and not with inner worship. Their inner process is to think and intend whatever is demanded of their outward nature. These are people who are caught up in worship of living or dead individuals and are therefore involved in the worship of idols and in belief in miracles." (Emanuel Swedenborg, *Divine Providence*, trans. George Dole [West Chester, PA: Swedenborg Foundation, 2003], §136:9). "Since foreknowledge of what will happen destroys our essential human nature, our ability to act in freedom and rationally, no one is allowed to know the future" (Swedenborg, *Divine Providence*, §179). "The apostolic church had been like a new star appearing in the sky. The church after the two Nicene councils was like the same star dimming and disappearing (a phenomenon that has in fact happened several times in the physical world, according to astronomers' observations)" (Emanuel Swedenborg, *True Christianity*, vol. 1, trans. Jonathan S. Rose [West Chester, PA: Swedenborg Foundation, 2006], §176). In this book, quotes from Swedenborg's writings will be cited by section number, which appeared in the original text and are uniform across all editions.

Ch. 1: Unity and Determination in Swedenborg

1. The existential label that we attribute to Swedenborg's thought is motivated by two aspects: phenomenologically, since Swedenborg, like those authors, considers the human being, as with all reality, to be in a state of open and constant otherness; in a vital sense, since for the Prophet of the North human beings need to direct themselves toward spiritual life and fulfillment in all its fullness, that is, humans show in their innermost specificity a desire for infinity that always projects it beyond (the *epektasis* of Gregory of Nyssa). In addition, and repeating the label of existential, Swedenborg likewise considers the crucial problem of those authors to which we alluded: his system arises from the intent of reconciling (speculatively and vitally) the fundamental oppositions of reality, so that unity saves the independent reality of the oppositions themselves.

2. It is thus established as a type of platonic example. But it is a dynamic example, since all tangible reality is led to join together (*conjunctivum*) with its archetype or celestial part. The correspondence between our world and the pleromatic or archetypal world makes each thing of our world possess an index of intelligibility or spirituality that is the sense of each thing. To

interpret or discover this figure is to elevate each thing to its pleromatic or spiritual correspondence. No citation for this is necessary, since it is illustrated throughout Swedenborg's work.

3. "Beyond this even, if you look at the functions of everything that has been created, you will see how they follow in sequence all the way to humanity and from us to our source, the Creator. You will see how the connectedness of everything depends on the Creator's union with us" (*Divine Providence* §3); "Our rational freedom comes from our being midway between heaven and the world" (*Divine Love and Wisdom* §142).

4. The *ratio illustrata* of Swedenborg, a motif that is repeated constantly, shows the rationalizing and apologetic intention that moves our author, without discrediting other tendencies. But the scientific spirit of the Enlightenment is present in all Swedenborg's work, as is demonstrated by the importance—for the totality of his system—acquired by his theory of the origin of the universe as stemming from the solar mass (and thence the great value given to heat and light as powers coming from the sun).

5. See Ch. Coulston Gillespie, ed., *Dictionary of Scientific Biography* (1970).

6. See Swedenborg, *Divine Love and Wisdom,* §223.

7. The importance of determination in Swedenborg's thought shows itself to us in the value of the action of the universal in the particular, which allows us to classify that thought under the term kathenotheism. The profound sense of kathenotheism is that in the constitution of the spiritual, no quantitative considerations enter in, but just the qualitative ones. Thus Swedenborg can affirm that an angel is the entire church, or the inverse, that God is everyone and in each one. This is the kathenotheism of which Corbin speaks: God is in each one by ontological multiplication, not by juxtaposed addition. The kathenotheism is verified in the wise Swede through the constant mention of the distributive *singuli,* equivalent to *káta* in the Greek. See *Divine Love and Wisdom* §79 and *Secrets of Heaven* §§5986 and 4329. "We can therefore tell that the Lord is heaven not only in a general way (for all who are there), but also specifically (for every individual who is there). An angel is actually a heaven in smallest form; and heaven in general is made up of as many heavens as there are angels" (Swedenborg, *Divine Providence,* §30). Therefore, we can speak of an authentic mysticism of determination. For the issue of kathenotheism, see Henry Corbin, *La paradoxe du monothéisme* (Paris, 1981); and *Temps cyclique et gnose ismaélienne* (Paris, 1982).

8. The universal analogy that involves correspondence and representation functions from the angel to the mineral, from heaven to humans. And inversely, there exists a tension from the spiritual conjunction of the inferior toward the superior. See *Divine Love and Wisdom* §§57, 227, 376.

9. In the faith-works polemic, Swedenborg was an advocate of the preeminence of works over faith. This posture of the Nordic thinker is understandable for many reasons. First of all, because of the priority that our author concedes to the affective and proactive instantiations versus the intellectual ones (and for him faith is an intellectual capacity, tied to understanding); secondly, because this proactive posture is above all metaphysical, therefore an ontological category has to be resolved in action in order to reach its fullness; thirdly, because of the pietistic influence. Eric Peterson considers Swedenborg's work as a pietistic criticism of orthodox Scandinavian Protestantism, and in this sense he places Swedenborg's work alongside of Kierkegaard's. See E. Peterson, *Tratados teológicos,* trans. Agustín Andreu (Madrid, 1966), 213 and Swedenborg's *Divine Love and Wisdom* §216 and *Divine Providence* §128.

10. For all this, see Henry Corbin, *Mollâ Sadrâ Shîrâzî. Le Livre de pénetrations métaphysiques* (Paris, 1964) and *L'imagination créatice dans le soufisme d'Ibn 'Arabi* (Paris, 1977); Miguel Asín Palacios, *El Islam cristianizado* (Madrid, 1981); René Guénon, *Les États multiples de l'Etre* (Paris, 1980); Eugeni d'Ors, *Introducción a la vida angelica* (Madrid, 1986).

11. The unitary and global vision of reality—spiritual as well as natural—where everything mutually corresponds and where everything progresses and returns *(progressio and reditus)* relates Swedenborg with the line of thought of Pseudo-Dionysius, Gregory of Nyssa, or Scotus Eriugena, except that the thought that underlies this conception in the Scandinavian is fundamentally of scientific origin. We have already mentioned the organic and vital evolution that enlivens all reality and that, according to Swedenborg, propels it toward the realization of its fullness: it is the *conatus* or vital force that internally moves nature to act. All this thought will influence the mystical and naturalistic currents of Romanticism, eager to find a vision that would reassemble the world in its unity and in which humans would find their own place in solidarity with the rest. The other affiliation in which we place Swedenborg— what we call existential—connects with the one just mentioned, and is given by the state of openness and of ontological noncompliance of humans.

Ch. 2: The Role of the Subject in Swedenborg

1. We could apply here the reflection of Hans Jonas about Pascal and the anguish of the modern human in the desacralized world. According to this line of thought, Pascal—like Swedenborg—would propose a rectification in the qualitative order of the subject and its functions. See Hans Jonas, *La Religión gnostique* (Paris, 1978), 420 ff. (the whole chapter "Gnosticism, Existentialism, and Nihilism" makes reference to what we are saying).

2. Let us not forget that one of the fundamental motifs of Swedenborg's thought lies precisely in the search for the point of union of the *res extensa* and the *res cogitans,* so that the spirit does not dissolve and annul itself in the *res extensa.* It is a matter of rehabilitating the role of the subject in the world, and essentially of reconciling the subject with the vision given by science (as is also, in certain measure, the issue for Pascal). Regarding this, see Lucien Golman, *La búsqueda de lo Absoluto (Le Dieu caché)* (Barcelona, 1968).

3. Again Pascal serves as a point of reference: "The eternal silence of those infinite spaces terrifies me" (*Pensamientos,* 206).

4. Unamuno shared this extreme and knew how to link it in a lucid fashion with Swedenborg in *Del sentimiento trágico de la vida.* See the section in this book titled "Swedenborg and Miguel de Unamuno."

5. Two opinions that are very pertinent to this issue are those of Titus Burckhart in *Ciencia moderna y sabiduría tradicional* (Madrid, 1979), and René Guénon, *El signo de los tiempos y el reino de la cantidad* (Madrid, 1976).

6. See Philo of Alexandria: *Fug.,* 12; *De Somn.,* II, 45; *Migr.,* 103: *Leg.,* 111, 96: *Heres.,* 230–31. In the Judaic tradition the image of the Macranthropos has a full development by means of the figures of Enoch, Adam Kadmon, Metratron. See G. Stroumsa, "Form of God: Some Notes on Metratron and Christ" *Harvard Theological Review* 76, no. 3 (1983): 269–88.

7. Emanuel Swedenborg, *Traité des Representations et des correspondances* (Paris, 1985), 45. For the Romantic treatment of Swedenborg, see Ernst Benz, *Les sources mystiques de la philosophie romantique* (Paris, 1964) and J. Roos, *Aspects litteraires du mysticisme philosophique* (Strasbourg, 1952). But to know the image that Romanticism had of our author, nothing better than the novel of Honoré de Balzac, *Seraphita.*

8. The nuptial symbolism throughout the entire Bible is very rich and always found in contexts which want to signify states of fullness, harmony, and happiness. See, among others, Revelation 21:2; Isaiah 61:10; Revelation 19:7–9; Matthew 22:2–3; Revelation 22:17; Hosea 2:19; Leviticus 5:34, and all the Song of Solomon. As for Swedenborg we would have to cite his work

Marriage Love (sometimes translated *Conjugial Love*) in its entirety.

9. It is not surprising that Swedenborg is interested in the book of Revelation, since here (as in all apocalypses) the religious categories of revelation—which is the meaning of apocalypse—and prophecy are synthesized. The religious experience of our author is determined precisely by an apocalyptic characterization, which is what configures that experience with its peculiar images. The revelation and prophecy of Swedenborg are, then, his own experience, his particular religious experience. It is a matter of fulfilled eschatology and his *Revelation Unveiled* consists of his interpretation of Revelation, and in this measure, apocalypse itself. Hermeneutics, apocalypse, and eschatology coincide in the kairotic moment of the revealing of meaning. See Henry Corbin, "La foi prophétique et la sacré," *Cahiers de L'Université Saint Jean de Jérusalem,* no. 3 (1977) and also his *Temple et Contemplation* (Paris, 1980), 409–417. José Antonio Antón-Pacheco, "El tiempo de la interpretación," chapter 4 in *Symbolica Nomina* (Barcelona, 1988), 183–217.

10. See C. G. Jung, *Psicología y Alquimia* (Barcelona, 1989), 19; *Paracélsica* (Buenos Aires, 1966), 24, 63 ff. The similarity between Paracelsus and Swedenborg is sometimes surprising. Paracelsus also speaks of a *homo maximus,* which he identifies with heaven and at the same time with *interior homo.* In this order of things we need to review the intelligent approach of the prestigious orientalist Heinrich Zimmer with his notion of Cosmic Human in Jainism and Brahmanism with their parallel Great Human in Swedenborg, clarifying the phenomenological correspondences between both mythic images. See Heinrich Zimmer, *Filosofías de la India* (Buenos Aires, 1979), 197–201.

Ch. 3: Hermeneutics and Inner Experience

1. For all these themes related to the notion of a revealed book, see our *Symbolica nomina. Introducción a la hermenéutica espiritual del Libro* (Barcelona, 1988).

2. Neither Antonio Orbe (*Estudios valentinianos,* vol. 5, Rome, 1955, ff; *Cristología gnóstica,* vol. 2, Madrid, 1976), nor José Monserrat Torrents (*Los gnósticos,* vol. 2, Madrid, 1983), mention exegesis as being among the key motivations of gnostic thought, although they do keep it in mind and the grant it its due importance. Neither does Hans Jonas (*La religion gnostique,* Paris, 1978), who doesn't appear to give it any importance at all.

3. It would be too much to extensively cite the great authority on this topic, Henry Corbin, given that all his works are in some way connected to

these issues. Since it makes reference to Swedenborg, we will cite here his fundamental "Herméneutique spirituelle comparée (II. Swedenborg, II. Gnose ismaélienne)," *Eranos Jahrbuch* 33 (1964): 71–176. This article was later published in the book *Face de Dieu, face de l'homme: herméneutique et soufisme* (Paris, 1983).

4. We call Swedenborg's *Secrets of Heaven* midrash in the same way that L. Alonso Schökel and E. Zurro have been able to speak of midrash in reference to Malón de Chaide, that is, as the development of variations around a scriptural theme. See *La traducción Bíblica: lingüística y estilística* (Madrid, 1977), 309. Regarding kabbalistic exegesis, see G. Scholem, *La Cábala y su simbolismo* (Madrid, 1978); *Les noms et les symboles de Dieu dans la Mystique juive* (Paris, 1977); Moshe Idel, *Language, Torah, and Hermeneutics in Abraham Abulafia* (New York, 1988).

5. See Henry Corbin, *Avicenne at le récit visionnaire* (Paris, 1979).

6. G. Brooke, "Qumran Pesher: Towards the Redefinition of a Genre," *Revue de Qumram* 40 (1981): 483–505.

7. See our *Testigos del instante* (Madrid, 2003), especially the chapter "Angelología, mediación e interpretación"; see also M. Cacciari, *L'Angelo neccesario* (Milan, 1986). Swedenborg himself says: "I have explained at some length in *Teachings for the New Jerusalem on Sacred Scripture* that in the individual words of Scripture there is something spiritual that expresses divine wisdom and something heavenly that expresses divine love, and that angels are aware of these when someone is reading the Word devoutly" (*Divine Love and Wisdom* §280).

8. We could apply here the words of Hamann: "All biblical narrative is a prophecy that is fulfilled throughout all the centuries and in each human soul."

9. Jacques Combes, *Le récit de la creation dans son sens interne. Concordance de Sainte Thérèsa d'Avila et d'Emanuel Swedenborg* (unpublished manuscript). I owe the acquisition of this work to the courtesy of the erudite Swedenborgian Karl-Erik Sjöden.

Ch. 4: Internal Time and Space

1. *La mano y el espíritu,* trans. Aurelio Garzón del Camino (Mexico, 1975).

2. See René Guénon, *El reino de la cantidad y los signos de los tiempos,* trans. Ramón García Fernández (Madrid, 1976). In fact, space is always con-

sidered qualitative space, and for consciousness a merely quantitative experience of spatiality is impossible (closely related is the notion of landscape). For an excellent synthesis of these issues see Mariano Ibérico, *El sentimiento de la vida cósmica* (Buenos Aires, 1946).

3. See Mircea Eliade, *Tratado de historia de las religiones* (vol. 2), trans. A. Medinaveitia (Madrid, 1974).

4. See Henri Bergson, *Ensayo sobre los datos inmediatos de la conciencia,* especially chapter 2.

5. See Jean Pucelle, *El Tiempo,* trans. E. Montaldo (Buenos Aires, 1976).

6. See Hans Jonas, *La religion gnostique* (Paris, 1978), 78–79; Antonio Orbe, *Estudios valentinianos II: en los albores de la exégesis Johanea* (Rome, 1955), 186–7. Likewise, my *Symbolica nomina,* p. 146 and all chapter 4.

7. See Henry Corbin, *L'Imagination Créatrice dans le soufisme d'Ibn Arabí* (Paris, 1976); also *Terre céleste et corps de résurection: de l'Iran Mazdéen à l'Iran shî'ite* (Paris, 1961). And, in general for all these themes, *En Islam Iranien,* vol. 4 (Paris, 1972).

8. See Henry Corbin, ed., *Sohravardî: l'Archange empourpré. Quince traités et récits mystiques de Sohravardî* (Paris, 1976).

9. We could compare this description of the intermediate spiritual world with a great number of cases; key examples include Plato's *Republic,* VII, 529; Plotinus, *Ennead,* VI, 7; Proclo, *Catalogue de manuscrita alchimiques gracs,* vol. 6 (Brussels, 1928); Sohravardi, op. cit., 374.

10. A constant of the spiritual currents of the eighteenth century and of Romanticism lies in the postulation of this inner church (the church of Saint John) versus the external church (of Saint Peter), of the church of the free spirit versus the church of the dogmas, and in this sense the influence of Swedenborg is decisive. See Jacques Roos, *Aspects litéraires du mysticisme philosophique* (Strasburg, 1951); E. Benz, *Les sources mystiques de la philosophie romantique* (Paris, 1961). In addition, the deep meaning of interiority in Swedenborg is not far from the *Glaubenslehre* of Schleiermacher: "The divine spirit is certainly the same in all believers, but it acts differently in each one and in each one its manifestation is distinct; the Divine Spirit always finds in each person an individualized reason." Cited by Pierre Demange in *Inspiration prophétique et foi chrétienn,* p. 28, in the already reviewed *La foi prophélique et la sacré.* It is also the case that Schleiermacher as well as the wise Swede were both influenced by the Moravian Brothers. And is Swedenborg's theological system a certain manner of intuition of the Infinite?

Ch. 6: The Two Forms of Religiosity in the *Journal of Dreams*

1. I cite the critical edition by Lars Bergquist, *Swedenborgs Drömbok, Glädjen och det stora kvalet* (Stockholm, 1988). Also I have utilized the French edition by Régis Boyer, *Le Livre des Rêves* (Paris, 1985). [Swedenborg wrote the dream diary in Swedish and never titled it, nor did he appear to have any intention that it be published. The most common English translations are *Swedenborg's Journal of Dreams 1743–1744* and *Swedenborg's Dream Diary*. In the original text of this book, the author refers to Swedenborg's dream diary as either *Drömbök* or *El Libro del los sueños;* in this translation we refer to the book throughout as *Journal of Dreams.*—ed.]

2. All these historical references can be found in the cited edition of Bergquist, which is very rich in informative notes.

3. [English translation for this and following passages taken from *Swedenborg's Dream Diary,* trans. Anders Hallengren, with commentary by Lars Bergquist (West Chester, PA: Swedenborg Foundation, 2001), 101. This is an English translation of the Swedish volume cited in note 1 above.—ed.]

4. Ibid., 169.

5. Ibid, 174–5.

6. *Nouvelles de la Republiques des Lettres I-II* (1986): 55–69.

7. Hallengren, *Swedenborg's Dream Diary,* 244–5.

8. Ibid., 118.

9. Gabriel Andreas Beyer (1721–99) was one of the first Swedish disciples of Swedenborg. He was a professor of Greek and lived in Gothenburg, where there was a small group of faithful followers of the teachings of Swedenborg. Friedrich Christoph Oetinger was one of the principal philosophers of German Romanticism and the first translator of Swedenborg into that language, which led to censorship by the government of Württemberg. In spite of his interest, Oetinger (who was a Lutheran pastor) remained distant from Swedenborg's ideas. Both letters can be found in A. Acton, ed., *The Letters and Memorials of Emanuel Swedenborg,* vol. 2 (Bryn Athyn, PA, 1955), 622–3. With respect to the Pauline fervor of Swedenborg, we must say that later on this evolved into theological positions that were more critical with respect to Saint Paul.

10. Hallengren, *Swedenborg's Dream Diary,* 207.

11. Ibid., 182. The bad syntactic construction and the continual stylistic errors of the original Swedish text emphasize his sincerity and spontaneity, and this is in our judgment a proof of its veracity.

12. Ibid., 185–6.

13. Ibid., 145–6.

14. We compare these fragments of Swedenborg: "I was in heaven, and I heard a speech that no human tongue can utter, nor can anyone describe the glory and bliss of that life. . . . To the highest be praise, honor, and glory! Hallowed be his name! Holy, Holy, Lord God Zebaoth!" (Night of April 5–6; Hallengren, *Swedenborg's Dream Diary*, 121) with these others of the *Memoire* of Pascal: "God of Abraham, God of Isaac, God of Jacob, not of the philosophers nor of the wise men. Certainty. Certainty. Feeling. Happiness. Peace. God of Jesus Christ" (Blaise Pascal, *Thoughts*). These words denote mystical experiences that are phenomenologically comparable. But this similarity between Swedenborg and Pascal is based not only on these inner experiences. There is between these two thinkers a common thread that ties them together: both are scientists that come to question the general vision that science of their time (fundamentally Cartesian) provided to reality. Both, impelled by desires and restlessness related to faith, need to go beyond their own scientific knowledge to access a transcendental dimension, as well as to reach a unitary and synthetic conception where the oppositions would become reconciled.

15. Hallengren, *Swedenborg's Dream Diary*, 103.

16. Ibid, 178.

17. As is known, in Eastern Christianity there is hesychasm, a tradition of breathing exercises in preparation for meditation. In addition, one can find studies on the notion of out-of-body experiences throughout the work of Mircea Eliade.

18. In this positive appreciation of the lack of literary style to judge mystical writings, we follow the criteria of Louis Massignon in his classic work *Expérience mystique et les modes de stylisation littéraire, Opera Minora*, vol. 2 (Paris, 1969). Massignon's methodology in analyzing mystical vocabulary as a source of spiritual meditation and devotion would also be applicable to Swedenborg.

Ch. 7: Representation and Concept

1. H. Jürgen Baden, *Literatura y conversion*, trans. Luis Alberto Martín Baró (Madrid, 1969).

2. There is a great phenomenological similarity between the figurative vision of Swedenborg and that of Sohravardi. In essence, in the Nordic thinker the notion of fantasy approaches the notion of Sohravardi of *bárzaj*,

that is, the limit that separates light from the darkness characteristic of contingent entities; since also for Swedenborg the principal characteristic of the deliquescent or fantastic realities is the darkness, versus the luminosity identified with representations. On the other hand, Sohravardi is also a philosopher who combines conceptual thought with narrative. Cf. Shihabuddin Yahya Sohravardi, *L'Archange empourpré. Quinze traités mystiques de Sohravardî, traduit du persan et de l'arabe par Henry Corbin* (Paris, 1976); *Le livre de la sagesse orientale (Kitab Hikmal al'Ishraq), commentaires de Qotboddîn Shîrâzî et Mollâ Sadrâ Shîrâzî, traduction et notes par Henry Corbin, établies et introduites par Christiann Jambet* (Lagrasse, 1986). Swedenborg would be by antonomasia a philosopher of the *mundus imaginalis* or transcendental imagination, thus the representative character of his discourse.

3. In this requirement of image and schematization in the elaboration of the philosophical discourse, Swedenborg coincides with the Spanish philosopher Eugeni d'Ors (1881–1954), who in his time wrote some intelligent notes about the Prophet of the North in *Introducción a la vida angélica*, 2nd ed. (Madrid, 1987).

4. Karl-Erik Sjöden, *Swedenborg en France.*

5. Miguel Florián, *Anteo* (Huelva, 1994). [Translated by Steven Skattebo.]

6. Jorge Luis Borges, "El otro, el mismo," in *Obra poética* (Madrid, 1972). [Translated by Steven Skattebo.]

7. Carlos Liscano, *Miscellanea observata* (Montevideo, 1995). The informed reader will appreciate the coincidence of the title with a work by Swedenborg of the same name. [Poem translated by Steven Skattebo.]

Ch. 8: Swedenborg in Hispanic Literature

1. *Obras completas,* vol. 3, ed. by Manuel García Blanco (Madrid, 1967).

2. Ibid., 200. Translation taken from Miguel de Unamuno, *The Tragic Sense of Life,* trans. J. E. Crawford Flitch (New York: Dover, 1954).

3. Ibid. (translation of J. E. Crawford Flitch).

4. In this sense, the studies of Henry Corbin, and more specifically the already cited "Hermenéutique spiritualle comparée (I. Swedenborg. II. Gnose Ismaélienne)" have been fundamental for a better comprehension of Swedenborg.

5. The phenomenology of the angel has been treated in depth by Corbin in multiple places, so I will not highlight them here. The same author has

accurately traced the spiritual affiliation to which Swedenborg belongs. It would be convenient to point out only that in this affiliation we find our Eugeni d'Ors with his book *Introducción a la vida angélica*.

6. *Obras completes*, 242 (translation of J. E. Crawford Flitch).

7. Ibid. (translation of J. E. Crawford Flitch). There is another explicit reference to Swedenborg, also citing *Heaven and Hell*, on page 240 of the book in question by Unamuno. We will not transcribe this reference *in extenso* because it does not bear directly on our topic. We do, however, want to acknowledge it.

8. Ibid., 253 (translation of J. E. Crawford Flitch).

9. Ibid., 259 (translation of J. E. Crawford Flitch).

10. *Introducción a la vida angélica*, ed. José Jiménez (Madrid, 1987). The first edition was published in Buenos Aires (Editoriales Reunidas, 1939).

11. *L'Homme de lumiére dans le soufisme iranien* (Paris, 1971).

12. "Necesité de l'Angéologie" in *Le Paradoxe du monothéisme* (Paris, 1981).

13. *Introducción a la vida angelica*, 14.

14. Ibid., 94.

15. See Karl-Erik Sjöden, *Swedenborg en France*.

16. However, Aranguren affirms that d'Ors held a great esteem to the Iranian way of life, although it seems to us there is a lack of mention of the Fravashi in his angelology. Undoubtedly the "classical" prejudices influenced this.

17. *Prólogos*, ed. Torres Agüero (Buenos Aires, 1975), 153–62. The prologue in question is the work *Mystical Works*.

18. *Borges oral*, ed. Bruguera (Barcelona, 1980). [An English version of this essay titled "Testimony to the Invisible" appears in James F. Lawrence, ed., *Testimony to the Invisible* (West Chester, PA: Swedenborg Foundation, 1995), 5–16.—ed.]

19. *Prólogos*, 161.

20. *Obra poética* (Madrid: Alianza Editorial, 1972), 222.

21. There is no work of Henry Corbin where Swedenborg is not mentioned, but his classic work on the Nordic thinker is the already cited "Hermenéutique spirituelle comparée (I. Swedenborg. II Gnose Ismaélienne)."

22. *Infierno*, trans. José Rodríguez (Barcelona, 1981), 185. For Strindberg, the hell described by Swedenborg was vivid because of its particular *descensus ad infieros*.

23. *Otras inquisiciones* (Buenos Aires, 1966), 137.

24. For Oswaldo Romero the Swedenborgian influence over the religiosity or spirituality of Borges is indisputable, as is explained in "Dios en la obra de J. L. Borges: su Teología y su Teodicea," *Revista Iberoamericana* (1977): 100–101. This is a monograph edition dedicated to Borges.

25. *Libro del cielo y del infierno* (in collaboration with Bioy Casares) (Barcelona, 1971), 40, 43, 61, 62, 155, 174. With respect to Heine, p. 107.

26. *Cuentos breves y Extraordinarios* (in collaboration with Bioy Casares) (Buenos Aires, 1967), 87.

27. *Obra poética, 255.* Given that it is a poem of thanksgiving to the "divine labyrinth of effects and causes," we can infer the importance of Swedenborg for Borges.

28. *La cifra* (Madrid, Alianza Editorial, 1982), 67. Could there be here some connection with Eugeni d'Ors? In this respect see his booklet *Oraciones para el creyente en los ángeles* (Valladolid, 1981).

29. "Jardines místicos" in *Jardines lejanos.* Edición del Centenario (Madrid, 1982).

30. Juan Ramón Jiménez read Swedenborg, as is demonstrated by a volume that is a part of his personal library in his museum in Moguer. The book in question is *Theology and Philosophy (The Divine Providence),* introduction by Howard Spelaing (London and New York, no date). Inside the book we find the signature of Juan Ramón and Zenobia and the date of 1920. Much later, then, than the first edition of *Jardines lejanos,* 1904.

31. We have a sample of this conception of language in Sebastián de Covarrubias: "So that the communication between the two (Adam and Eve) from then on was by means of a language which was not acquired nor invented by them, but rather influenced by The Lord and with so much correctness that the names Adam gave the terrestrial animals and the birds fit them perfectly, because knowing their qualities and properties, he gave each one of them what was essentially appropriate . . . but after the flood, with the confusion of languages, that one was forgotten, remaining in one family, that God reserved for the rest . . . which were called Hebrews, and their language Hebraic." Prologue to *Tesoro de la lengua castellana o española,* edition of Martín de Riquer (Barcelona, 1987).

32. [The quote in the Spanish edition does not appear to exist in Swedenborg; in this text we substituted a passage of similar meaning. A direct translation of the original quote follows.—ed.] "They told me (the angels) that the first language that humans spoke on our planet was of nature itself, since it came from heaven, and they added that the Hebrew language

matches with the language of heaven in certain respects. All the names in Scripture signify things and are changed in heaven to the ideas of the things that they mean."

33. An enumeration of all of them is beyond our scope. For an intelligent presentation of the theme, we refer to Antoine Berman, *Le préuve de l'étranger* (Paris, 1984); Georges Gusdorf, *Les origines de l'herméneutique* (Paris, 1988); Isidoro Reguera, "La teoría del lenguaje en M. Roso de Luna y Bover: la cuestión del lenguaje primitivo o del origen del lenguaje" in *Mario Roso de Luna. Estudios y opinions,* ed. Esteban Cortijo (Cáceres, 1989).

34. See also *Secrets of Heaven* §§2896, 2686, 2897, 10355, and 10632.

35. *Hieroglyphic Key* is the title of a book of Swedenborg written during his scientific stage (the manuscript dates from 1741; it was published posthumously in London in 1784), which shows that the interest of the wise Swede for themes of a theological-linguistic tone was one he had held for a long time. In this work Swedenborg attempts to give an interpretive key to the analogies among the different divine, natural, and human symbolisms (considered to be the traces of an original language), that is, he attempts the configuration of a *mathesis universalis* (in this Swedenborg is not far from the influence of Wolff and Leibniz). In fact, the structure of a *mathesis universalis* as a common code for all the studies of reality is one of the central projects of Swedenborg's work. Significantly, Hamann, who uniquely joins hermeneutics and existential problems, speaks likewise of hieroglyphs: "To speak is to translate . . . from one angelic language to a human language, that is from thoughts into words, from things into names, from images into signs, which can be poetic or kiriologic, historic or hieroglyphic, philosophical or characteristic" (*Aestetica in nuce,* translation, introduction, and notes by Henry Corbin in the monograph of *Cahier de L'Herne,* dedicated to Corbin, [Paris, 1970], 196). In the same vein, Theodore Ranke states: "Each action gives a testimony to Him, each instant announces his Name, above all, it seems to me, the articulation of the aggregation of history. He is present as a sacred hieroglyph" (letter to Heinrich Ranke, cited by Gusdorf in *Les origines de l'herméneutique,* 23).

36. As he affirms in the introduction to Juan Ramón Jiménez, *Selección de prosa lírica* (Madrid, 1990), 57; and also in the introduction to Juan Ramón Jiménez, *Antología poética* (Madrid, 1987), 80.

37. I cite Juan Ramón Jiménez through the edition of Agustín Caballero, *Libros de poesía* (Madrid, 1979).

38. See also *Secrets of Heaven* §§1641–45, 4609, 7089.

39. See also *Secrets of Heaven* §§1008, 1869, 4946, 6613–18, 10355.

40. We focused on this theme in "Juan Ramón, Espacio, Píndaro" in *Capela*, no. 2:13 (1982): 4–8. See also Eliacer Cansino, "Lectura hegeliana de Juan Ramón Jiménez" in *Er, revista de filosofía*, I (1985): 43–51.

41. I owe the information on the Swedenborgian influence in María Zambrano to Alicia Sánchez Dorado, author of an undergraduate thesis about the writer from Málaga, who provided me with the details of the Swedenborgian presence in Zambrano.

42. The Spanish volume is translated by Adelina Núñez de Baker and published by the Swedenborg Foundation, New York, 1946.

43. For more on Andersen and the Swedenborg Society of Spain, see the following section.

44. Alicia Sánchez Dorado, "María Zambrano y Emanuel Swedenborg," *Boreas* 3 (2003): 47–62.

45. See the earlier sections on Unamuno, d'Ors, Juan Ramón Jiménez, and María Zambrano. There is an article by Gonzalo Fernández de Mora with a promising title: "La recepción krausista de Swedenborg" in *Razón y libertad. Homenaje a Millán-Pueyes*, coordinated by Rafael Alvira (Madrid, 1990). It would seem that it might address the penetration of Swedenborgian ideas in Spain through the influence of Karl Christian Friedrich Krause. However, we found nothing of this in the cited article. On the contrary, it is completely tendentious and it lacks any intention of understanding, interpreting, or revealing of what could be the true sense of Swedenborg's thought. It is a diatribe in which details are distorted and decontextualized. It is all directed towards the true objective of Gonzalo Fernández de la Mora (it is neither Swedenborg nor Krause that ultimately interests him): denigrate Sanz del Río and Spanish Krausism.

46. I dearly thank the whole family of Jörgen Hartvig Andersen and especially his grandson Christen Blom-Dahl for all the assistance that they provided me while I was doing this research. Without their willingness, my study would not have been possible.

47. Neither in the General Archive of the Administration (Alcalá de Henares), nor in the Delegation of the Government of the Valencian Community, nor in any other place have we found testimony or documentation of the SSS, which leads us to believe that Andersen never bothered to legalize the society. The only official document of Andersen's Swedenborgian activities is the inscription with the number 33737 in the Facultative Corps of Archivists, Librarians, and Archaeologists, for the registry of the intel-

lectual property of his translation of *La Verdadera Religión Cristiana* (*True Christianity*, Valencia).

48. It seems that a Rowlan Lees, textile engineer and resident of Cieza (Murcia) and Barcelona during the 1930s, collaborated with Andersen in the SSS. However, there is no record anywhere of just what this collaboration could have been. Rowlan Lees was born in 1874 and died in Manchester in 1957. He was an active member of the North of England New Church (an institution charged with spreading the writings of Swedenborg) and founding member of the Manchester Swedenborg Association. Andersen, at his death, donated a large part of his library to the General Conference of the New Church (then in London) through Lees. Currently that library is found in the headquarters of the North of England New Church House (Manchester). I thank the helpfulness of the Reverend A. Arnold and of Miss Anne Casell (of the New Church College) for supplying me this information.

Let us now examine very briefly the books that Andersen donated at his death. There were various copies of his Spanish translations of Swedenborg's works; a complete collection of HNC (however, this last collection is not part of the list that the Reverend A. Arnold supplied me); works of Swedenborg in English; the *Swedenborg Concordance* of J. F. Potts; various titles of theologians of the New Church, such as Giles, Mitchel, Hyde, Schick, George Jr., Presland, Acton, Hite, Smyth, all in English (from this collection Andersen extracted his material for translating in the HNC); an edition of the *Essays* of R. W. Emerson; various books in Swedish, and among them various editions of Swedenborg, which is interesting because it shows that Andersen must have contrasted the English and Swedish versions for his Spanish versions. The Swedish editions in Andersen's collection were: *Arcana Caelestia* (*Secrets of Heaven*), *Om Nya Jerusalem och dess Himmelska Lära* (*On the New Jerusalem and its Heavenly Doctrine*), *Den Gudonliga Kärläken* (*The Divine Love*), *Kort Framställning af Läran för Nya Församligen* (*Brief Exposition of the Doctrine of the New Church*).

49. For the reader to have a complete idea of the Swedenborgianism of Andersen, we include here the epigraphs of these instructions for the faithful of the New Church: "1. What is the New Church? 2. From what source is the Church derived? 3. What is the central teaching of the word according to its interior light? 4. What relation does Emanuel Swedenborg have with the New Church? 5. What is religion? 6. What is life? 7. What is the human? 8. What are the centers of action? 9. Why are we born first in a body of flesh

and blood in a material world? 10. What fact with respect to the first birth makes it necessary that we be born again so that we can enter the Kingdom of Heaven? 11. What is salvation? 12. Why is it divinely ordered that humans work for their own salvation? 13. In the opposition of the spiritual mind to the natural mind, which is subordinate? 14. What use does prayer have? 15. What are the laws of order? 16. What is sin? 17. What is repentance? 18. What is forgiveness? 19. What is the Word? 20. How is the internal or spiritual sense related to the external or literal sense? 21. What is the law of symbolism? 22. Why is symbolism known as another name? 23. Is knowledge of correspondences necessary for understanding Scripture? 24. How does the knowledge of correspondences remove the darkness from the Bible in what it teaches with respect to the Second Coming of the Lord? 25. What are, in summary, the Doctrines of the New Jerusalem?: a) The Doctrine of the Lord; b) The Doctrine of the Sacred Scriptures; c) The Doctrine of Life; d) The Doctrine of Faith."

50. As we stated earlier, an exception must be made with the dissemination work of the Mexican physician L. E. Calleja, who beginning in 1898 translated the works of Swedenborg into Spanish. Unfortunately, all his translations remained unpublished. His manuscripts are found currently deposited in the Swedenborgian House of Studies at the Pacific School of Religion, a college of theology at the University of California, Berkeley.

51. Andersen was in contact with the General Conference of the New Church (London), as shown in his correspondence with the president of said church, the Reverend S. J. C. Goldsack, with the secretary of missions for Europe, O. E. Prince and with J. R. Presland. Another proof of this is that Andersen donated part of his library, upon his death, to the General Conference through Rowlan Lees.

52. We have only been able to locate numbers of the HNC in the Municipal Newspaper Library of Madrid (and only a few of them) and in the Archive of the Civil War in Salamanca (also just a few and misplaced in a bundle which is a collection of documentation of Protestant confessions. The HNC found there must have belonged to the Theosophical Society of Madrid, since they carry their stamp). This generalized absence denotes the lack of social penetration from which the HNC suffered. In the private library of the Andersen family we have volumes 2, 3, and 4 of the HNC. Volume 1, as with the rest of the translations published in book form, are found in the Royal Library of Stockholm and in the University of Uppsala Library ("Carolina Rediviva"), naturally together with the rest of the HNC.

Andersen was in charge of sending all the publications of the SSS to those two prestigious Swedish libraries.

Ch. 9: Relationships and Influences

1. Bergquist, *Swedenborg's Dream Diary*, 103, 142, 173, 182, 193, 225.

2. Bergquist, *Swedenborg's Dream Diary*, 121.

3. These would be: a collection of manuscripts published posthumously under the title of *Ontologia* (*Ontology,* commentaries on the philosophical lexicon of Wolff, an unpublished manuscript written around 1742), *De Commercio animae et corporis* (*Soul-Body Interaction,* 1769) and *De Athnasii Symbolo* (*On the Athanasian Creed,* a mostly theological work, written in approximately 1760). We exclude the scientific texts, nearly all of which belong to the first phase, but some to the second phase (in contrast to what is usually believed, in his mystical phase Swedenborg wrote as many as eight scientific, economic, and technical works).

4. As can be shown, it is equivalent to the Soul of the platonic world, cf. my article "El Alma de mundo y la naturaleza" in *La Naturaleza y el Espíritu,* ed. A. López Tobajas and María Tabullo (Barcelona, 2006).

5. Curiously, Raimundo Lulio says that he coined the terms *"bonificar–bonificable–bonificado"* [not easily translatable: goodify–goodifiable–goodified] according to the *modum loquendi arabicum.* See Tomás Carrera y Artau and Joaquín Carrera y Artau, *Historia de la filosofía española,* vol. 1 (Madrid, 1939), 510 ff. Also, in a special manner, Pablo Beneito, *El lenguaje de las alusiones: amor, compasión y belleza en el sufismo de Ibn 'Arabi* (Murcia, 2005), 79.

6. In this entire exposition we are indebted to Henry Corbin. Also, it should be stated that the theory of the Names of God as personal pronouncement and revelation of God himself is profoundly rooted in the biblical world.

7. Ibn 'Arabi, *El secreto de los nombres de Dios,* introduction, translation, and notes by Pablo Beneito (Murcia, 1997). See also Pablo Beneito, op. cit.

8. We see this, for example, in the early work *Height of Water* (Uppsala, 1719). We could easily generalize to the rest of his scientific works.

9. This is what I have attempted to show in my books *Symbolica Nomina. Introducción a la hermenéutica espiritual del Libro* (Barcelona, 1988) and *Testigos del instante. Ensayos de hermenéutica comparada* (Madrid, 2003). All this essential linkage of figurative thinkers with the interpretation of the Sacred

Book is the consequence of the fact that hermeneutics itself is derived from the practice of exegesis of revealed texts, something that no historian of hermeneutics is willing to grasp (only a few brief and insufficient allusions to Philo of Alexandria). A recent work that serves as an example is an excellent synthesis by Modesto Berciano: "Inflexión de Heidegger en la historia de la hermenéutica" in *Studia Philosophica* III (Oviedo, 2003), where in a brief overview of the history of interpretation there is no mention at all of the decisive contributions of the exegesis of the Revealed Book. On the contrary, we believe that the fundamental concepts of hermeneutics are not *Auslegund, Verständnis, Nachkonstruiren,* or *Gefüh,* but rather midrash, *Haggadah, tafsir,* or *taw'il.* Likewise, the true advocates of contemporary hermeneutics are Massignon, Corbin, and the Eranos group.

10. This notion seems fundamental, precisely because it delimits, separates, and differentiates each thing as it is.

11. Other symbols of special relevance in Ibn 'Arabi are, for example, the Cloud or the Tree of the World (another image equally of a great universal and traditional whole).

12. An interesting analysis of the idea of protohuman in Swedenborg is found in Lars Bergquist, *Ansiktets ängel och den stora människam* (Stockholm, 2001).

13. *Regnum Animale* (1744–45) is the title of the last great work of the scientific phase of its author, but the issues posited here have their continuation in the visionary and theological phase, but only approached from the spiritual perspective.

Ch. 10: Swedenborg and Romantic Religiosity

1. We now give a general bibliography, but one that is valid for all the themes treated in this article. This exempts us, then, from having to repeat it. Brian Juden, *Traditions Orphiques et tendances mystiques dans le Romantisme français (1800–1955)* (Geneva–Paris, 1984); Ernst Benz, *Les sources mystiques de la philosophie romantique* (Paris, 1961); J. Roos, *Aspects litteraires de mysticisme philosophique et l'influence de Boehme et de Swedenborg au début de Romantisme: Blake, Novalis, Ballanche* (Strassburg, 1951); Karl-Erik Sjöden, op. cit.; Auguste Viatte, *Les sources occultes du Romantisme, Iluminisme, théosophie, 1770–1820,* 2 vols. (Paris–Geneva, 1979); Albert Beguin, *El alma romántica y el sueño* (Madrid, 1978); Paul Benichou, *El tiempo de los profetas. Doctrinas de la época romántica.* (Mexico, 1984).

2. See Emil Leonard, *Historia general del Protestantismo*, 4 vols. (Madrid, 1967); Leszeck Kolakowski, *Cristianos sin iglesia. La conciencia religiosa y el vínculo confesional en el siglo XVII* (Madrid, 1983). For us Miguel Servet would be a paradigm of this attitude.

3. In fact the most well-known books on alchemy are more modern than anything else: *Las doce llaves de la filosofía* by Basilio Valentín; *La entrada abierta al palacio cerrado del Rey* by Ireneo Filaleteo; *Filosofía natural restituida* by J. d'Espagnet; *Las doce puertas de la Alquimia,* by Georges Ripley, etc. (there are Spanish translations of all of them). See Alexander Koiré, *Místicos, espirituales y alquimistas del siglo XVI alemán* (Madrid, 1981). Alchemy and the occult sciences were enormously popular in modern Spain, as is demonstrated by their constant presence in all Spanish literature of the Golden Age. Torres Villarroel is a representative figure in this regard. See J. García Font, *La Alquimia en España* (Madrid, 1976); Juan Eslava Galán, *Cinco tratados españoles de alquimia* (Madrid, 1987).

4. See Antoine Faivre, *El esoterismo en el siglo XVIII* (Madrid, 1976); René Le Forestier, *La Franc-Maçonerie occultiste et Templière aux XVIII et XIX sieclés* (Paris, 1970). In J. B. Willermoz we find a faithful representative of all these tendencies: in him Herrnhutism and French Masonry are joined.

5. The body of literature, all the theories and ideologies that lead to investigations of the Revelation or the Origin as a source of myths, symbols, religions, and language is immense, qualitatively and quantitatively. If we had to trace a line of thought, it could be this: Kircher, Curt de Gebelin, Vico, Herder, Creuzer, and so on, giving rise to Fabre d'Olivet, Ballanche, Saint-Martin, Senancour, etc.

6. See Antoine Berman, *Le preuve de l'etranger. Culture et traduction dans l'Allemagne romantique* (Paris, 1970). The book of Fabre d'Olivet, *La langue hébraique restitueé* (Paris, 1816–17), is a clear exponent of the mystical concept of language. Some authors and fundamental works for this issue of language and of primitive poetry are Robert Lowth, *De sacta Poesi Hebraeorum* (Oxford, 1753) (interestingly the French translation of this book was carried out in the press of Ballanche in Lyon, 1812) and the *Essai sur la langue et la philosophie des Indiens* by Friedrich Schlegel, French translation appearing in 1837.

7. Swedenborg himself wrote a *Clavis Hieroglyphica Arcanorum Naturalium et Spiritualium per Viam Representationum et Correspondentiarum (A Hieroglyphic Key to the Secrets of Material and Spiritual Things by Way of Representations and Correspondences;* London, 1784) (published posthumously).

Romantic examples of these repertories of universal symbols and of their revelations are, within the Swedenborgian sphere, the *Dictionnaire mytho-hermetique* by Antoine Joseph Pernety (Paris, 1758), the famous champion of the Iluminati of Avignon; and the *Essai d'un Dictionnaire de la langue de la Nature, ou explication de huit cents images hyeroglyphiques* (Paris, 1831), by the abbot J. G. E. Oegger.

8. Henry de Lubac, *La posteridad espiritual de Joaquín de Fiore. De Joaquín a Schelling* (Madrid, 1989). The Romantic personality that best embodies the spirit of social reform united with the mystical spirit is Pierre Simon Ballanche; see his *Oeuvres completes*, 6 vols. (Paris–Geneva, 1967). Let us remember, in addition, that Fourier was profoundly influenced by Swedenborg.

9. We need not insist on the repercussion that this preference for the supernatural has on the utilization the literature refers to. By means of example, see Manuel García Viñó, *El esoterismo de Bécquer* (Sevilla, 1991).

10. The kabbalah is Christianized, and in a way is popularized after the Renaissance with Pico de la Mirándolla, Reuchlin, and Guillermo Postel, but it is with *Gate of Heaven* (Amsterdam, 1655, although the Spanish manuscript is earlier) by Abraham Cohen de Herrera, and *La Cabbala denudata* (Sulzbah, 1677–84), by Knorr Von Rosenroth, when he is fully introduced into the modern era. See also M. Secret: *La Cábala cristiana en el Renacimiento* (Madrid, 1979). From the explanation of the kabbalah as a restorative hermeneutic come thinkers such as Hamann, Walter Benjamin, or Gershon Scholem. See G. Gusdorf, *Les origines de l'hermenéutique* (Paris, 1988). See also my books *Symbolica Nomina* and *Testigos del instante*.

11. From this point of view, Swedenborg would be placed together with Hamann or Schleiermacher, that is, in the line of a restorative hermeneutics of sense. See Henry Corbin's already frequently cited "Hermenéutique spiritualle comparée (I. Swedenborg; II. Gnose ismaélienne)" in *Face de Dieu, face de l'homme: hermenéutique et soufisme* (Paris, 1983); G. Hamann, *Aestetica in nuce*, translation and notes by H. Corbin in the monograph of *Cahier de l'Herne* dedicated to Corbin (Paris, 1970). Hamann is a pre-Romantic author who joins spirituality, hermeneutics, and experimentation with language in an interesting fashion.

12. The most extensive was the *Abregé des ouvrages d'E. Swedenborg* by Daillant de la Touche (Strassburg, 1788).

13. For Swedenborg's own descriptions of the ages of the world, see *True Christianity* §§202, 760, 762:1 and *Secrets of Heaven* §§1114–1129; for his

description of the Most Ancient Church, see *Marriage Love* §77 and *True Christianity* §§3, 279. For Henry Corbin's interpretation, see op. cit. and *Temple et Contemplation* (Paris, 1980), 409–417. For a comparison of this Swedenborgian conception with *The Ages of the World* by Shelling, see Friedemann Horn, *Schelling and Swedenborg* (West Chester, PA: Swedenborg Foundation, 1997). For a commentary on the idea of a lost original Scripture in the center of Asia, see Anders Hallengren, *Magna Tartaria Hemlighet*, *Världarnas möte* 3 (1992): 104–23.

14. *Delitiae Sapientiae de Amore Conjugiali* (*Marriage Love*, Amsterdam, 1768). Another member of the Illuminati of Avignon, the abbot Brumore, made an adaptation of this book: *Traité curieux des Charmes de l'amour conjugal dans ce monde et dans l'autre* (Berlin–Bale, 1784).

15. Occultism itself is a typically modern phenomenon consisting in encasing spiritual categories and notions in supposedly scientific (or scientifist) molds, giving rise to a species of positivism of the spirit. For a clear analysis of this phenomenon, cf. René Guénon, *Le Théosophisme, histoire d'une pseudoreligion* (Paris, 1965); *L'erreur spirite* (Paris, 1952). The "Swedenborgian" works of Balzac, especially *Louis Lambert*, suffer from that occultist vision. Likewise it occurs in the *Inferno* of Strindberg, a book also dripping with Swedenborgianism.

16. This occurs, for example with "literary Swedenborgianism" (cf. Ana Balakian, *El movimiento simbolista* [Madrid, 1969]), that is, with the utilization of elements taken from Swedenborg with a literary purpose, as with the *Aurelia* of Nerval.

17. Eric Peterson, *Kierkegaard y el Protestantism, Theological Treatises* (Madrid, 1966).

18. Nevertheless, Emerson's criticism of Swedenborg is based on the excess of representation and figuration of Swedenborg's proposals in the theological sphere. Cf. R. W. Emerson: "Representative Men," in *Essays and Lectures* (New York, 1983). On this same topic, but in a more positive sense, see Czeslaw Milosz, "Dostoevsky and Swedenborg," *Slavic Review* 34 (1975): 302–18.

19. *Revue des Sciences Religieuses* 2 (1993): 55–74.

Ch.11: Some Reflections

1. Lars Bergquist, *Swedenborg* (Uppsala, 1986).

INDEX